THRIVING MARRIAGES

2nd edition

THRIVING MARRIAGES
2nd edition

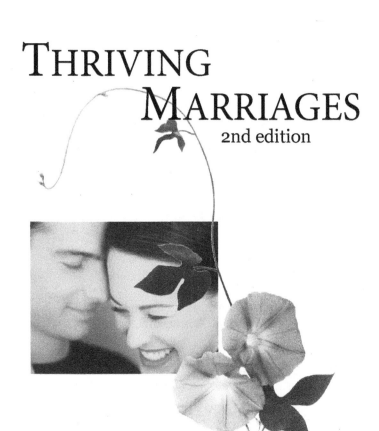

An Inspirational and Practical
Guide to Lasting Happiness

JOHN YZAGUIRRE, Ph.D. and
CLAIRE FRAZIER-YZAGUIRRE, MFT, M.Div.

New City Press
of the Focolare
www.newcitypress.com

Published in the United States by New City Press
202 Comforter Blvd., Hyde Park, NY 12538
www.newcitypress.com
©2015 John A. Yzaguirre, Claire Frazier-Yzaguirre

Cover design by Michele Wetherbee
Cover photo: © Nonstock / Pure
Used with permission

Library of Congress Cataloging-in-Publication Data:
    Yzaguirre, John A.
    Thriving marriages : an inspirational and practical guide
to lasting happiness / John A. Yzaguirre, Claire Frazier Yzaguirre.
    p. cm.

    ISBN 1-56548-194-1
    1. Marriage. 2. Couples--Psychology. 3. Love. I. Yzaguirre, Claire
Frazier.
II. Title.

HQ734.Y93 2003
646.7'8--dc22   2003066466

1st Printing: January 2004
Second Edition - First Printing: August 2015
            ISBN 978-1-56548-591-4

Printed in the United States of America

Contents

Introduction

Introduction to Second Edition

Since our first publication of *Thriving Marriages*, we have given seminars on its content to over 300,000 people across the United States. Two areas emerged that needed further clarification and elaboration: how to make conflict resolution more effective and how to communicate our needs more clearly. As a result, we have rewritten Chapter 10: Solving Conflicts with Wisdom and Respect. The new chapter simplifies the conflict resolution process focusing on the role of Understanding, Validating and Acting, which we refer to as the UVA response. This type of empathic response allows people to integrate their differences and transform the conflict into an opportunity to grow in their unity. The chapter also includes a new questionnaire which covers the skills required and can be used as a tool to engage in constructive dialogue.

Our new Chapter 10 elaborates on the role of assertiveness in a process defined as "interpersonal coaching" which shows how to communicate more clearly the ways in which we would like to be treated without resorting to using such aversive and ineffective approaches as venting, complaining or criticizing.

The feedback from the participants in our seminars consistently revealed that the other chapters of the book remain relevant, inspirational, practical and effective as they were originally written. Our desire is for you the reader to use this book as a helpful and concrete guide to transform your marriage into a thriving, resilient and compassionate journey of lasting happiness.

For those of you involved in Marriage and Family Life, Religious Education, and Adult Faith Formation ministries, we invite you to include this new edition of *Thriving Marriages* in your curriculum and ministries as well as our different audio formation materials that accompany it and can be found on our website:

www.ThrivingFamilies.com.

Introduction to First Edition

How does this book differ from the many others on marriage? It presents a new model of the dynamics of unity for a Christian marriage; a clear methodology to implement it; a way that couples from different Christian denominations and cultural backgrounds can apply it; and finally, a non-technical approach that is relevant, inspirational, practical, and effective.

Most books about marriage present principles, skills, or habits drawn from research as well as a "recipe" for a lasting relationship. They often lack a clear model for a healthy and happy marriage. This book presents a model of Christian marriage that integrates the best psychological findings on successful marriages with a contemporary spirituality of Christian unity. We have written the book as if we were having a conversation with you, avoiding clinical language. The Appendix contains some additional resources about married life.

An anecdote might help present our model. Claire found a card that said on its cover: "There are three important ingredients for a successful relationship." With great curiosity, she opened the card. Inside, she read, "Unfortunately nobody knows what they are!" We laughed because we could have supplied the list. Our model presents three dynamics of unity in a marriage: empathy, autonomy, and mutuality.

Our methodology reveals a strategy for developing empathy, autonomy, and mutuality. They represent the three basic dimensions of a marriage: your spouse, yourself, and the relationship between the two of you. Empathy allows you to get to know your spouse; autonomy is the gift of self that you bring to the relationship; mutuality is the relationship that emerges from a creative synthesis of empathy and autonomy. When a couple develops, integrates, and lives these dimensions their marriage becomes a loving and joyful experience of unity in diversity.

First, we present *empathy as intelligent love.* Empathy allows spouses to know and love each other in a meaningful and relevant way. It is the art of welcoming each other into their lives. Empathy does not depend on whether they love each other but whether they feel loved the way that they want to be loved. The more a partner feels understood, accepted, valued and loved, the more likely that he or she will reciprocate. True empathy leads to mutuality, not to codependency. Empathy is a set of skills. We will explore how partners can connect emotionally with each other (chapter 1); how to understand each other's needs (chapter 2); how to respond to those needs intelligently (chapter 3); and we will conclude with a reflection on the soul of empathy (chapter 4).

The second part of the book proposes *autonomy as the gift of a healthy self.* Autonomy means that spouses take adequate care of their individual lives to become the best personal gift for each other. Visualize life as a home with seven rooms: work, family, friends, soul, health, education and community. We will offer strategies to bring harmony to each "room" of your home and achieve balance in life (chapter 5); powerful antidotes for the "toxic" thoughts that distort reality and trigger negative feelings (chapter 6); practical ways to simplify and de-stress life (chapter 7); and conclude with a reflection on the soul of autonomy (chapter 8).

Part 3 presents *mutuality as the joy of unity.* Perfect love is mutual love. Empathy is altruistic love: spouses loving each other unconditionally. Autonomy is maximizing the ability to love. Through mutuality, mature love reaches perfection. The process of mutuality involves the art of communicating with each other (chapter 9); the ability to solve conflicts with wisdom and respect (chapter 10); the power to forgive and reconcile (chapter 11) and living a spirituality of unity (chapter 12).

The book also contains questionnaires and exercises that identify and fine-tune these skills. We invite spouses to fill them out and to put them into practice. This book can help partners draw a personal blueprint for the marriage they desire. Every marriage is a "work in progress" and applying these exercises and strategies will allow partners to actualize the potential that lies hidden within their relationships. Dedicate one week to applying the skills in each chapter of the book, and in three months you can celebrate abundant new life in your marriage.

This book reflects our unique ecumenical and cross-cultural background. John is Catholic and when we met and married, Claire was an ordained American Baptist minister. John comes from a Hispanic background and Claire comes from an Anglo-American background. Our families of origin differed markedly. Yet, over the years we have applied what we talk about in this book and although we experience the same shortcomings and setbacks as any other couple, we enjoy a thriving marriage. Experience has shown us that our model applies to couples from different Christian denominations and cultural backgrounds.

We believe that you will find this book relevant to your own marriage, whether you are newly married, "empty-nesters" or celebrating a golden anniversary or beyond. We hope that it will inspire and motivate you to practice the strategies that we suggest, and that your marriage will reach a new level of unity, as have countless other couples. The feedback that we receive from the work-shops and retreats on marriage and family life that we present across the country underscores the positive impact of this model on lives and marriages. It has helped couples transform their marriage from mere survival or maintenance into a journey of continuous growth. The simplicity of the vision that we propose and the practicality of its approach can transform your marriage into the one that God wishes for both of you.

Our spiritual integration of the dynamics of unity stems from the Christian perspective that we try to live, but we are convinced that other faith traditions also offer valuable insights on the spirituality of marriage. If you are not a Christian we invite you to select those principles that you find consonant with your beliefs.

This book can be a blueprint for building your marriage day by day. It provides both a unified vision and the essential skills necessary to make that vision a reality. Do not read this book once and put it on a shelf, but keep it handy as a mini-reference of skills that you can practice for the rest of your life.

Part 1

*E*mpathy: Intelligent Love

Without a doubt you love your partner, but does your partner feel loved by you the way that he or she wants to be loved? The greater your empathy, the stronger the love that your partner will experience from you. Empathy is called "intelligent love" because it is an eminently thoughtful way for partners to relate to one another. It has three dimensions. The first, connecting emotionally with your partner, is activated when you love with your heart, showing emotional sensitivity towards your partner's feelings. The second, understanding your partner's needs, is activated when you love with your mind revealing your insight into your partner's current needs underneath his or her feelings. And the third, loving your partner intelligently, is activated when you respond to your partner's needs with concrete and relevant action. This final and most critical step in empathy makes your love visible and real to your partner. Empathy skills will transform you into a sensitive, understanding, and responsive lover and will set a solid foundation for all the other skills that we present in this book.

1. Connecting Emotionally with Your Partner

When we see couples, we often ask about their "empathy quotient." One response, especially vivid, stands out. Claire asked a husband: "Please tell me, what makes your wife genuinely happy?" Irritated, he replied: "That's what I'm paying you for! You tell me what makes her happy because after so many years I still don't know!" Obviously you do not need to pay a therapist to discover what makes your partner happy, but perhaps you do need to change strategy. Maybe you think that the less upset, or less worried or less depressed that your partner becomes, the happier he or she will be. Experience suggests that this is not so. Happiness is not the absence of something negative but rather the presence of something positive. You can help your partner become happier by providing the positive and meaningful experiences that he or she wants from you.

Three basic skills will increase the emotional connection with your partner: make room for your partner in your heart, become interested in how he or she is feeling, and validate his or her feelings. Whenever you see a little box with the heading: "Try this" practice what it suggests. These simple, effective exercises will strengthen your empathy skills.

Make Room for Your Partner in Your Heart

This is the art of welcoming your partner in your heart. Over the years you might have grown so accustomed to your partner's presence that now you might take him or her for granted or simply tolerate his or her idiosyncratic behaviors. One husband described this bluntly: "Now when I get home my dog is the only one who seems excited to see me!"

The starting point in empathy is treasuring your partner. Take a few seconds to focus on those qualities and strengths that you honor and respect in your partner. Focusing on your partner's existing positive attributes versus his or her negative traits restores your partner's value in your heart. Do this every day on your way home from work or as you prepare to meet again in the evening. When you greet your partner let him or her feel that you are glad that he or she is in your life. Often you can communicate this with a genuine smile and some expression of affection. Make him or her feel welcomed in your heart.

Joe, a successful physician, and Sylvia, a marketing executive, complained about their unfulfilling marriage and stressful lives. The more they talked, the clearer it became that they were living parallel lives. There were no nasty arguments or abusive behaviors, but both spent most of their time and energy in their individual careers. Their first challenge was to switch the focus away from themselves and onto each other. They acknowledged that they were taking each other for granted and their primary interest was not so much to love each other but to succeed professionally. Their jobs got the best of them and they ended up giving each other the leftovers. Fortunately, they were willing to focus first on each other's feelings and needs. This meant a change in their priorities and to practice daily the art of welcoming each other into their hearts. Today they feel far more emotionally connected and happier, and their professional life has benefited as a result.

Try This

When you get home from work,
look your partner in the eyes
and make him or her feel welcomed into your heart.

Become Interested in How Your Partner Is Feeling

Remember when you were dating your partner? You had an insatiable curiosity about how he or she was feeling. Over the years you may have shifted focus away from your partner and more towards yourself. Perhaps now you expect that he or she will be available for emotional support as needed, and hope that he or she will not interfere with your plans. When you disregard your partner's feelings as unimportant, however, you are actually disregarding your partner. Understanding your partner's feelings opens the door into his or her intimate emotional life. Perhaps you find yourself operating in a task-oriented mode. From the beginning of their marriage, many couples define and assign each other roles and focus on fulfilling those duties in order to be a good husband or wife. This would be true if marriage were only a legal contract, but marriage is more than a division of labor. It is a sacred covenant in which the principal rule is to love one another. The rest follows as a consequence.

One feeling deserves special attention: finding out what makes your partner happy. You do not have to be particularly insightful or sensitive to notice what makes your partner angry because sooner or later he or she will tell you. This applies also to what makes your partner worried or depressed. In more than twenty years of clinical experience with couples, we have found that most people are only partially accurate, uncertain, or even dead wrong about what brings their partners genuine happiness.

Mary and Robert had been married for seven years. She complained that Robert liked to run the household as if it were his office. He was caring and responsible but always placed tasks before people. He was convinced that he was a good husband because he worked very hard to provide for his family and had never cheated on his wife or done anything immoral or illegal. He could not understand why Mary was unhappy with him. After all, he thought, wasn't he hardworking, loyal, honest, and responsible? Mary eventually confronted him: "Yes, Robert you have all those qualities, but you don't give me what I want!" Throughout their marriage he played the role of the good husband, *according to him!* Finally, he realized that he was a good husband only if Mary felt loved by him. Mary wanted a husband that focused first on loving her and the kids and then on completing tasks. He also discovered that Mary felt loved by him when he understood and valued her feelings.

Try This

Once a week, ask your partner
for something specific that you could do
during that week to bring him or her joy.

Validate Your Partner's Feelings

Validating your partner's feelings means valuing how he or she is feeling and showing it through supportive feedback. You do not need to analyze or judge the validity of those feelings but simply appreciate that he or she shared them. Now you can understand and support him or her in a better way.

Mark and Tiffany had difficulty validating each other's feelings. Their attempts to communicate with each other usually followed a predictable pattern of failure. When Tiffany shared anger, worry, or sadness, Mark tried to help her by offering advice on how to solve or prevent the situation that caused those negative feelings. He did not validate her feelings first by saying something such as: "I can see how upsetting that was for you. Is there anything that I can do to help you now?" Often Tiffany just wanted to feel understood. Whenever Mark gave her unsolicited advice, she became upset with him for patronizing her or disregarding how she felt. Mark, in turn, felt upset that she did not appreciate his genuine desire to help with her problem and began to withdraw emotionally. Tiffany felt his detachment and began to resent and criticize his emotional insensitivity and shared her feelings again only with reluctance. This aversive cycle continued until it became unbearable.

Fortunately they broke the cycle by learning to validate each other's feelings. Now their sharing leads to greater emotional intimacy.

Try This

When your partner shares feelings with you,
value what he or she shared, without offering solutions
or unsolicited advice.

---

2. Understanding Your Partner's Needs

The second dynamic of empathy is to understand what your spouse needs to feel loved by you. Most couples spend their days working away from each other. Needs and feelings change every day and, unless a partner volunteers that information, there is no way for one spouse to know what the other needs without asking.

Feelings cluster into four basic categories: happiness, anger, anxiety and depression. We feel happy when our needs are met in the present; we feel angry when our needs or wants are not met in the present; we feel anxious when we fear that our needs will not be met in the future; and we feel depressed when we experience significant losses or feel helpless about fulfilling unmet needs.

Feelings and needs are deeply connected. When your partner is feeling angry he or she needs your understanding; when your partner is feeling anxious, he or she needs your reassurance; when your partner is feeling depressed, he or she needs to be comforted; and when your partner is feeling happy, he or she needs to share that joy with you! Each one of us is unique in how we feel and how we meet our needs. There is no "one size fits all." You need to find out from your partner his or her specific needs at any particular moment.

Many couples that have been married for a number of years have fallen into the illusion of believing that they know each other's needs when in reality they are just assuming them. Their inability to understand and respond to each other's needs brings them to therapy. With deep sadness, we have listened to many a spouse express dissatisfaction with a partner who for many years has acted faithfully and responsibly but has failed to love in a meaningful and relevant way. There are three ways to promote understanding: ask your partner what he or she needs from you, acknowledge and accept those needs, and respond with attention, affection, and appreciation.

Ask Your Partner What He or She Needs from You

The best way to find out what your partner wants or needs (if he or she has not told you), is to ask. Do not try to guess. Misunderstanding leaves unnecessary emotional scars. Instead, ask your partner directly what specific behaviors he or she expects. For example, if your partner says that she needs you to be more supportive, ask her: "in what specific ways would you like me to show you my support?"

In our marriage, we have found it a great advantage that Claire was born and raised in California and John was born and raised in Spain. Being aware of our cultural differences prompts us to tell or ask each other what we want in a genuine desire to understand our different backgrounds and expectations. Our ongoing interest and assertiveness spares us from unnecessary false assumptions and subsequent dissatisfactions.

It is dangerous to assume that if your partner does not communicate any needs it means that his or her needs are being met. No news is *not good news*. Some partners stop complaining not because their needs have been met, but because they have become disillusioned and emotionally detached. In their silence, they may be contemplating a way out of an unfulfilling marriage.

Try This

Find a moment to ask your partner about what he or she needs the most from you this week.

Understand and Accept Your Partner's Needs

Another obstacle to understanding your partner's needs may be your own unrealistic expectations. You might expect that your partner should be your emotional manager or personal cheerleader. When you come home from work you may expect that he or she should welcome you and take care of you. This is unrealistic because it assumes that your partner does not need anything from you and has not faced his or her own stress, difficulty, or pain during the day. It is more realistic to return home ready to accept what your partner might be feeling and needing in that moment. In other words, love your partner as he or she is, not a fantasy version of him or her.

Paul complained that whenever he got home from work, Ruth bombarded him with the kids' most recent crisis and put him to work around the house. Unrealistically, he expected to come home to a happy wife who would leave him alone to relax after a long day. Ruth expected that Paul would return home full of energy, ready to help her with the kids and chores. Paul wanted a relaxed and cheerful wife. Ruth wanted an energized and helpful family man. These ideal expectations could be fulfilled on some days, but more often than not both had had a demanding day and it would have been more realistic for them to accept and help each other. When they replaced their unrealistic expectations with genuine understanding and acceptance of each other's daily needs, their relationship became more real and rewarding.

Try This

When you get home from work, accept your partner's needs and help him or her concretely.

Respond to Your Partner with Attention, Affection, and Appreciation

Your partner has three essential needs: attention, affection, and appreciation. They are easily taken for granted or neglected but they are like powerful antioxidants that keep your relational immune system strong and healthy. When you practice them, your partner will experience that he or she is the most important person in your life; that he or she is lovable; and that he or she is very special to you.

Lupe felt that Tony was a hardworking family man. Tony was proud of his professional accomplishments and considered himself a faithful and responsible husband. Nevertheless, Lupe's dissatisfaction with their marriage convinced him to come for counseling. When she expressed her unhappiness, he took offense and blamed her for their problems. According to him, she did not seem to value what he did for her. It took a while to calm him down so he could really listen to her. When asked what she wanted the most from him, Lupe replied: "I want to feel important, loved, and valued. I have already told him that I value his faithfulness, hard work, and dedication to our family." Tony had not given Lupe what she wanted and needed the most: attention, affection, and appreciation. He began to invest daily in the "triple A" of empathy and both saw their relationship begin to turn around. Not all couples respond to therapy successfully, but if you apply these skills consistently, you will experience a fundamental difference in your marriage.

Try This

Each day, find an opportunity to give your partner attention, affection, and appreciation.

---

3. Loving Intelligently

Connecting emotionally with your partner and understanding his or her needs leads to the third and most important dimension of empathy: loving your partner the way he or she wants to be loved. Once you know what your partner wants, give it to him or her with no strings attached. This is the most intelligent way to love your partner since you can be certain of what he or she wants or needs in that moment. Your actual behavior makes your love real. For example, many married people say that they would feel happier if their partner communicated more or better; others wish that they could enjoy more activities as a family; still others thirst for a deeper spiritual connection. Do not assume or guess. Ask your partner what he or she wants. If you answer that need with concrete and relevant actions, you will increase your joy as a couple.

We cannot emphasize enough the importance of this final step. It is tempting to feel comfortable when *you* know that you care for or understand your partner, but unless you show concretely that you are willing to provide what he or she wants from you, your love remains invisible. Anyone can learn the skills of empathy. Practice them every day, and you will discover, as have many other couples, gradual but definite improvement in your marriage

Love is real when it is concrete and visible. Nothing is small or insignificant if it is done out of love for your partner. Here are three ways to make your love intelligent, real, and timely: love your partner the way he or she wants to be loved, be concrete and realistic in your response, and help without being asked.

Love Your Partner the Way He or She Wants to Be Loved

You may feel comfortable loving your partner the way that comes naturally to you, or the way that you think you ought. If it is not what your partner wants, however, you are wasting your time and energy. Your partner will feel truly loved when you treat him or her the way that he or she wants to be treated. Your partner is the only expert on how he or she wants to be loved. You must be attentive and responsive. Marriage is not about proving what a great lover you are but about making sure that your partner feels loved.

Carl and Barbara came for therapy with very little hope for their marriage. He had been having a long-term affair, and when she found out about it she was hurt and visibly angry. He convinced her to come to therapy in a desperate attempt to save the marriage. Towards the end of the first session she stepped out for a moment. While she was gone Carl said, "I know it looks hopeless but I have an idea that will change her heart. From now on, every morning I will wake her up with the music that she likes, light her favorite aromatic candle, and serve her breakfast in bed until her heart softens up." John asked, "How do you know that's what she wants?" He replied, "Any woman in her right mind would love that!" John reminded him that they were talking not just about any woman, but about Barbara. He suggested that Carl check with her first. When Barbara returned to the room he shared his plan for saving their marriage. Indignant, Barbara fumed, "I don't give a damn about the candle, the music, and the breakfast in bed. I don't want food, candles or music. I want a husband who comes home directly from work, who loves his family and is faithful!" She then shared specific behavioral changes that she wanted. He decided to give her what she wanted. Several years later, they are still married because both have learned to practice this all important dimension of empathy.

Try This

Give your partner what he or she wants.

Be Concrete and Realistic in Your Response

Sometimes you know what your partner wants but you don't communicate clearly how much you can do and when you can do it. Every time you don't follow through on something you have agreed to do, you lose credibility, trust and respect. It is better to promise less and be specific about what you are willing or capable of doing, than to promise more and fail to deliver.

Nicole and Al were really stuck when they came to see Claire. Nicole was getting tired of asking Al to finish a house project that he had started months previously but had never completed. Whenever Nicole mentioned the house project Al responded defensively with excuses and promises. Nicole grew impatient and disrespectful and began to describe him as "unreliable," "incompetent," and a "procrastinator." Al acknowledged that he promised more than he could deliver in order to please her, but did not want to hire someone else to finish the job. Claire asked him what he realistically could accomplish, and he estimated that within 30 days he could finish a fourth of what he had originally promised. Nicole accepted his new promise but remained skeptical. With a realistic goal before him, Al finished the first part of the job in two weeks. He then promised another 25% and completed it earlier than expected. Two months later the entire project was done. He was amazed at the positive impact that it had not only on the house, but also on their relationship. He learned to respond to Nicole's expectations in specific and realistic terms and she learned to respect him in a new way.

Try This

Respond to your partner's needs in concrete
and realistic ways.

Help Your Partner Without Being Asked

Perhaps the greatest obstacle to empathy is remaining passive, and not showing that you care about your partner.

Some people are passive because they are afraid of making a mistake, some because they like staying in their own comfort zone, others as a form of indirect hostility. If you tend to be passive, acknowledge the root of your passivity and counteract it with acts of initiative. If you are passive because you fear disapproval or rejection, focus instead on making sure that you give your partner what he or she really wants. If your passivity stems from the psychological inertia of doing only what takes no thought or effort, remind yourself that you grow as a person when you make valuable choices and practice new behaviors. The relationship with your partner follows the same principle; it grows when both of you try new behaviors out of love for each other. If your passivity is your way of showing indirect hostility for something that your partner has done to upset you, remember that withholding love is like digging a hole that will drain the very life out of your relationship.

Martha refused to talk because Tom had failed to do something that she asked him to do. She had not communicated clearly how important it was for her, and in response he took offense at her giving him the silent treatment. Their relationship suffered periodically from this destructive cycle. Learning to take the initiative in understanding each other's expectations allowed them to guide their relationship away from the quicksand of passivity.

Try This

Take the initiative every day in offering help
to your partner.

---

4. The Soul of Empathy

The inspiration to practice empathy wells up from your soul. At a turning point in his life, John discovered the deep source of true empathy.

I remember as if it were yesterday a powerful experience I had when I was a teenager. I was searching for the true meaning and purpose of my life. A friend had invited me to hear a physician share how he was trying to live the gospel. At the end of the meeting I asked him if he really believed in all that he had talked about. He replied, "Who cares?" He then added: "The issue is not whether I believe in the gospel but whether you do." Sensing my struggle, he pulled out a prescription pad and wrote the following sentence from the gospel: "I tell you solemnly, insofar as you did this to one of the least of these brothers of mine you did it to me" (Matthew 25:40).

After giving me this unusual "prescription," he said, "For the next two weeks, live these words as if they were true, and then call me." I did, and my life has never been the same since that time. Before that meeting I valued people according to their intellectual abilities, physical attributes, social skills, emotional sensitivity, personal achievements, economic power, or other personal characteristics. Since that meeting, living those words of the gospel has made me realize the true dignity of each person and the treasure hidden within them: Jesus. It became real to me that Christianity was not about idealistic or romantic feelings of love, but about concrete acts of love for God and for the person next to me in the present moment.

One day I was sharing this experience at a couples' seminar and a man from the group told me: "It all sounds fine and dandy, but you haven't met my wife. There is no way you would see Jesus in her. " He mistakenly assumed that I was talking about an unusual mystical vision, not about the concrete experience of God's presence that we can have when we love others. Jesus himself promises: "To those who love me...I will reveal myself to them" (John 14:21). Jesus makes his presence known after we love him.

The comment from that man who could not "see" Jesus in his wife reminded me of an explanation attributed to Michelangelo. He was asked, "How do you transform a rock into a masterpiece?" He replied, "I remove what does not belong to it." On a human level, we usually see only the "rock" in others, but if we let the Artist live within us, with strokes of empathic love we can help him remove from our partner or our neighbor whatever is not important and liberate the masterpiece that is imprisoned within them.

We are fortunate that Jesus has already told us that when we will meet him face to face he will ask us how we have loved him in our neighbor. In other words, the ultimate test of a successful life is how well we have practiced empathy: our ability to respond to the needs of others in a relevant way. Empathy has eternal consequences.

What is the soul of empathy in your marriage? Loving Jesus in your spouse. When you are aware that Jesus lives in your partner, you realize his or her actual dignity and treat him or her with the utmost care and respect.

Jesus presents one of the clearest descriptions of empathy in the story of the Good Samaritan (cf. Luke 10:30-37). The Good Samaritan went out of his way to care for a stranger who had fallen prey to robbers and was left half-dead. He understood the stranger's needs and loved him concretely by dressing his wounds, bringing him to an inn on his own beast, and caring for him. He even asked the inn-keeper to care for him while he was gone and paid his expenses. His genuine compassion for that person in need motivated his acts of empathy.

The heart of empathy is compassion. Jesus taught us to become empathic, to love every neighbor that we meet concretely, even our enemies. On the cross, he showed us the measure of our empathy: willingness to lay down one's life for others as he did. The spiritual and psychological dimensions of empathy resemble one another. First make room in your life for your partner, then try to understand what your partner needs, and finally love him or her concretely and meaningfully.

In the moment when you are trying to love your partner, the first step is to make room in your life by emptying your mind, heart, and soul of anything concerning you, and paying total attention to him or her. If you are empty of yourself, your partner can express clearly what he or she wants or needs from you. This is what Jesus did when he made room for us in his life. Scripture says that he emptied himself: "Though he was in the form of God, he did not deem equality with God something to be grasped at. Rather, he emptied himself and took the form of a slave, being born in the likeness of men" (Philippians 2:7).

This is a difficult step because it requires self-denial. It is a positive choice to become nothing in order to receive everything that your partner wants to give you. The paradox of empathy is that if you become nothing out of love, you will experience the paschal mystery of passing from death to life because you have loved. Becoming nothing (emptying yourself completely) feels like dying, but if you do it out of love for your partner, it generates a new life in you. Jesus said that those who choose to save their life will lose it, but those who lose it for his sake will save it (cf. Mark 8:35). Paradoxically, you will discover that *you are when you are not;* you *are* when you love. To love means to die to oneself in order to live for the other.

The second step in the process of empathy is to identify with your partner's feelings and needs as soon as he or she starts telling you what is happening in his or her life. Make those feelings and needs yours. Understand what your partner wants or needs from you. Become one with your partner. The apostle Paul described how a Christian becomes one with others: "I have made myself all things to all people" (1 Corinthians 9:22).

The third step in empathy is to respond to your partner's needs in a concrete and relevant manner. Give your partner not what you think that he or she needs but what he or she is asking from you. The real problem here is that we like to decide for our partner and we resist being told what to do. However, love is real when it becomes a concrete and relevant act of self-giving. Jesus wants us to love with the measure of giving our lives, and that includes any legitimate request from your partner. The process of empathy starts with emotional sensitivity that leads to understanding your partner's needs and results in concrete acts of love that respond to those needs. *The soul of empathy is love for Jesus in your partner.*

Try This

Love your partner as you would love Jesus.

Review your empathy skills by answering the questions on this Empathy Skill Questionnaire. Any skill that receives a 3 or less is a good place for additional practice.

EMPATHY SKILLS QUESTIONNAIRE

Please circle the answer which best describes how
often you practice the following skills:

> 1 = Never
> 2 = A little
> 3 = Sometimes
> 4 = Pretty much
> 5 = A lot

1) I make sure that my partner feels
   loved by me   1 2 3 4 5
2) I ask my partner about his or her
   feelings   1 2 3 4 5
3) I validate my partner's feelings,
   without giving advice   1 2 3 4 5
4) I ask my partner about his or her
   needs   1 2 3 4 5
5) I understand and accept my partner's
   needs   1 2 3 4 5
6) I give my partner the attention
   that he or she wants   1 2 3 4 5
7) I give my partner the affection
   that he or she wants   1 2 3 4 5
8) I give my partner the appreciation
   that he or she wants   1 2 3 4 5
9) I love my partner the way he or she
   wants to be loved   1 2 3 4 5
10) I take the initiative to love
   my partner concretely   1 2 3 4 5

Part 2

Autonomy

5. The House of Self

Imagine that your life is a house with seven rooms: your family, job, soul, friends, health, on-going education, and community. They are not listed in order of importance, but each room is essential and interconnected with the others. The goal of this chapter is to take a virtual tour of your "house of self" and see how you can make your life more beautiful and welcoming by taking care of each room and creating a balanced life. When you balance your life, you give the gift of a healthy *you* to your partner. This strategy involves answering four questions:

1) What would you like to improve? (Your vision)

2) Why is that important to you? (Your motivation)

3) How are you going to do it? (Your strategy)

4) When are you going to do it? (Your time commitment)

The answer to the first question is your vision of how to make that area of your life more attractive. It should be a **positive vision** of how to promote beauty and growth, not a negative vision of how to remove "clutter" or avoid something negative.

The answer to the second question is your **personal motivation** for implementing your vision. It should be based on your personal values, not on your fears, or on some external reason that does not reflect your internal set of values (like getting your partner off your back). Own your choice 100%.

The answer to the third question is your **realistic strategy** for making it happen. It should be specific, within your possibilities, and should follow gradual steps.

Finally, the answer to the fourth question is your **time commitment**. It should allocate specific times in your schedule that will be dedicated only to implementing that decision. It becomes part of your new lifestyle.

You can use the following guide to fill out your answers according to the seven rooms of your house and periodically update it.

MASTER PLAN FOR THE HOUSE OF SELF

	Vision "What do I want to improve?"	Motivation "Why do I want to improve it?"	Strategy "How am I going to improve it?"	Priority "When am I going to improve it?"
Family				
Job				
Soul				
Friends				
Health				
On-Going Education				
Community				

Your Family

Let's start the tour of your house of self with this room. You will find many suggestions in this book for improving it because the model for creating unity as well as the skills that we are presenting can be applied to your family life as well. Families today come in all shapes and forms, but they all share a commitment to building loving relationships. Think of your family as a system of delicate interactions that requires continuous care and growth. Which ones require more attention at this time? What improvements would you like to target? The following exercise is a brief outline of the four criteria necessary to make a good change: vision (what), motivation (why), strategy (how), and priority (when).

Try This

Write your answers in your master plan:
What would you like to improve
about your family life?
Why? How? When?

Example:

What: I would like to increase our family time

Why: Because I want to promote family unity

How: We will set aside an evening a week for enjoyable family activities

When: On Saturday evenings (with everyone's agreement)

Take a look at the different roles and rules in your family and see if you need to change some of them or to create new ones to improve cooperation among family members. Think of your extended family and decide which relationships need your greater investment. How about the level of hospitality towards friends and others? This book presents numerous ideas on how to improve family life; focus on one at a time and make changes that last.

Your Job

For many people, this is the largest room in their house of self. We spend more time and energy in this area of life than any other. Some people let their job or professional achievement define their self-esteem and purpose in life. The challenge here is to work in a meaningful field that best uses your talents and benefits society. Then you must decide how many hours to spend in your job to maintain a balanced life. Once you have a clear picture of where to work and for how many hours, take a closer look at what professional skills need further improvement to do your job better.

We experienced a major shift in our lives when we decided to make a change in this area.

> I was working as a psychologist in a large healthcare organization and enjoyed the services that I could provide to people of all ages from a wide range of conditions. Feedback from my patients and recognition from the staff was rewarding. But there was a big problem — I worked far too many hours responding to contin-

uous emergencies and never knew when I was
going to get home from work. The one predictable aspect of my job was the high level of stress
and fatigue. It consumed most of my time and
energy. One night we discussed the long hours
and we agreed that I should work 40 hours a
week. The organization did not accept my
request for a less intense work schedule so I
decided to change jobs. It was the best decision
that I could have made because I got my life back.
My new job became the development of the California Prosocial Institute in partnership with
Claire. We were able to dream and bring to life
what we really wanted to do. Now, part of our
work is devoted to therapeutic services that we
enjoy offering. Increasingly though, our prevention and formation programs are becoming more
and more significant. Currently, across the U.S.,
30,000 people a year participate in our programs.
We have also become consultants to many
churches, agencies and organizations dedicated
to all forms of family ministry. When I resigned
from my previous job I did not anticipate the new
professional horizons and personal enjoyment
that would come as a result of balancing my life.

When you think about your job, make sure that you are
working in the right position and for the right amount of
time. Take a look at what you would like to improve. If
you are a parent who has chosen to stay at home, you can
apply this strategy to managing your household.

Try This

Write your answers in your master plan:
What would you like to improve
about your job?
Why? How? When?

Example:

What: I would like to be more focused at work
Why: Because I want to be more efficient
How: I will prioritize the most important tasks at work
When: Each day before I start working

Perhaps you need to cooperate more with your colleagues, or to redefine your job responsibilities by sharing or delegating some tasks, or to improve your time management skills, or to develop a new project. Think of what you could do to improve the quality of your performance, the level of satisfaction of the people that you serve, the innovation in what you do, and the relationships with your co-workers.

An important area related to your job is how you use money. Do you have a budget? Do you live within your means? How can you improve your financial management?

Your Soul

This is the most important room in your house of self. It holds your greatest treasure: God. Taking care of this room means paying attention to your relationship with God and how God wants you to treat others. In this place you find your true identity, the root of your self-worth, the meaning and purpose of your life. You can make this room more beautiful by identifying ways to improve your relationship with God. In chapter 8 we will present several suggestions.

Try This

Write your answers in your master plan:
What would you like to improve
about your spiritual life?
Why? How? When?

Example:

What: I would like to deepen my relationship with God
Why: Because I love God
How: I will meditate for 30 minutes each day
When: At 6:00 AM

Margaret was anxious and restless. She complained constantly about her demanding job, stressful family life, and her numerous physical ailments. We worked on cognitive behavioral strategies that she could use to cope with her anxiety, manage her stress, and improve her health. This approach helped, but she improved most when we addressed her spiritual needs. She decided to set aside time each morning for Christian meditation. Gradually she became more focused and learned to control her thoughts and feelings. Her spiritual gains improved her physical health. She is discovering that taking care of this room of her house daily is having a great positive impact on the rest of her life.

Your Friends

The hallmark of a real friendship is mutuality. Friends are important not simply because they can help each other in time of need, but above all because friendships allow us to develop our true self. You can discover who you really are when you are able to give yourself to others in a deep and transparent manner. This can happen with friends because they accept and value you as you are and give you honest feedback. The mutuality of friendship provides the psychological safety that is necessary to express your inner self.

How many close friends do you have? How much time do you spend interacting with them regularly? Most people fall short of the seven to ten close friends that studies suggest we need to be healthy and to cope successfully with illness and major life stressors. Your true "net worth" is your "network" of friends. E-mail, cell phones, and video technology keep making it easier to connect with our friends when we cannot meet with them in person. Take a look at the time, energy, and skills you invest to strengthen or develop new friendships every week.

Try This

Write your answers in your master plan:
What would you like to improve
about your friendships?
Why? How? When?

Example:

What: I would like to strengthen my friendships

Why: Because I value my friends

How: I will initiate sharing with _____ by phone,
          e-mail or in person

When: At least once a week, generally on Sunday after-
          noon

Your Health

Health depends not on how much you know but how
well you have integrated healthy habits into your lifestyle. Every day we are bombarded with information
about how to eat, exercise, and reduce risks to our
health. Examine how you care for your physical needs.
In chapter 6 we will also consider mental fitness.

You are probably confused by the conflicting information about diets. Your health depends upon good nutrition, not the latest diet. Studies suggest that healthy
nutrition includes:

• At least 5 servings of fruits and vegetables every day

• 8 glasses of water every day

- Whole grains, cereals, pasta, and breads
- Fish rich in omega-3 fats at least 3 times a week
- Red meat no more than 3 times a week
- 20 to 30 grams of fiber every day
- Foods low in fat, sodium, and sugar
- Avoiding partially hydrogenated fats
- Limiting or eliminating caffeine, alcohol, and soft drinks

Do you have room for improvement? Select one item at a time and incorporate it into your lifestyle. Watch the amount that you eat or drink. Last year we switched from drinking several cups of cafè latte a day to drinking water and green tea. Not only did we feel better physically, but we used the money we saved to buy a new projector for our seminars.

How often do you exercise? You do not need to join a gym or invest in expensive equipment to start and maintain an exercise program that includes:

— *Stretching exercises* to decrease muscle tension, increase flexibility, maintain joint mobility, improve circulation, and prevent injury. Stretch during the warm-up and cool-down periods before and after your other physical exercises.

— *Aerobic exercises* to strengthen the cardiovascular system and increase stamina. These might include brisk walking, jogging, bicycling, dancing, swimming, house cleaning, or gardening.

— *Strength training exercises* to strengthen muscles and protect joints. These may include weight lifting, crunches, push-ups, and squats. Before starting any exercise program consult your doctor to verify the frequency, intensity and duration appropriate for your current health status.

How much sleep do you need? Most adults need an average of 8 uninterrupted hours. What is your average? You may be able to increase your sleep by watching less TV or spending less time on the internet.

Target nutrition, exercise, sleep or any other health area in order to integrate permanent changes into your lifestyle. The goal is not to make temporary adjustments or cosmetic changes but to maximize physical energy and to enjoy continuous good health. The key to success is to initiate gradual and realistic changes and to maintain them.

Try This

Write your answers in your master plan:
What would you like to improve
about your health?
Why? How? When?

Example:

What: I would like to increase my physical fitness

Why: Because I value my health

How: I will walk for 30 minutes each day

When: At 7:00 AM

Frank considered himself healthy. He exercised regularly and usually ate nutritious meals. However, he coped with stress by munching sweets or by surfing TV or the internet when he got home from work. The extra pounds he put on triggered some painful childhood memories, when his weight had made him an easy target for ridicule. He described surfing TV or the internet as "a waste of time" that made him feel drained and sleep deprived. He began practicing stress management techniques, replaced junk food with healthy snacks, and invested the time that he wasted watching TV in family activities. Eventually he averaged 8 hours of sleep per night. By implementing these minor changes, he enjoyed major gains in self-confidence, self-image, and overall health. Now he controls his stress instead of letting the stress control him, and he and his family enjoy each other more!

Ongoing Education

Many things you learned during your formal education may well have become obsolete. New information and constant technological advances require a constant updating of our professional knowledge. For some this might mean pursuing a more advanced or a new degree, but for most this will take place through other forms of formal or informal on-going education.

Consider the seminars, on-line learning opportunities, books, tapes, videos, or coaching that you could use to update your knowledge. Often these activities aim to enhance professional skills but they could also expand your familiarity with subjects that interest you. Some people in technical fields like to learn more about history, literature, theology, the Bible, other cultures, other languages, or special hobbies. Feeding your mind with knowledge improves both your mind and your actions.

Try This

Write your answers in your master plan:
What would you like to improve
about your on-going education?
Why? How? When?

Example:

What: I would like to learn more about the Bible
Why: Because I want to enrich my faith
How: I will attend a Bible Study group
When: On Wednesdays from 8 to 9 PM

Your Community

You are a member of different communities: your neighborhood, city, county, state, country, and the human family. In every context, small or large, you are vital and irreplaceable. You have a personal contribution to make in all of them.

Some people become involved in a community agency or program whose cause appeals to them, often as a volunteer. Some people volunteer in outreach ministries through their local church. Others invest their talent and resources promoting justice and peace nationally or internationally. The possibilities are endless. Nobody else can give what you can. Whenever you give of yourself to help others in need you make a difference.

Example:

What: I would like to help the hungry in my community

Why: Because I care about them

How: I will volunteer through my church or community agency

When: On Sunday morning

Maintaining Your Balance

To balance your life you need three key time management skills:

1. *The big picture:* Setting personal goals that reflect your values.

2. *Your life rhythm:* Making a weekly schedule that reflects your goals.

3. *Enjoying life:* Living in the present moment according to your schedule.

The first step in time management consists in getting **the big picture** of your life: you have just looked at the seven rooms of your house of self and are deciding what is important to improve in each room. Life is not just about managing tasks, but about managing your time according to your values. In this step, define your personal goals. You can set short-term goals every month and long-term goals every year. The goals are the improvements that you have identified as your vision. For example: To strengthen my friendships.

The second step is to establish **a life rhythm**: a weekly schedule that allocates appropriate time for each room. This master schedule has only seven entries: these seven areas of your life. Each area requires a different amount of time. Some areas require a daily entry; others need to be scheduled once a week. This schedule is not a list of "To do" items but rather the rhythm of your life. It allows you to focus on what is important and to promote continuous and balanced personal growth. Revise it once a week if needed. *The key is to make sure that you invest in all areas every week.* Experiment until you determine the right amount of time needed for each category. It is like fine tuning an instrument before and after you play it. Every month or so, you can review your weekly schedule and make the necessary adjustments. Post your weekly schedule in a visible place until you memorize it, or carry it with you in your daily planner.

Sue and Don were having a tough time connecting through their busy schedules. They felt they were running through an endless list of tasks, missing the best part of their lives: enjoying each other and their two kids. They made a breakthrough when they made a "30-30-30 Daily Plan." They scheduled 30 minutes of meditation (spiritual fitness), 30 minutes of exercise (physical fitness), and 30 minutes communicating with each other (emotional fitness). It might seem that there isn't enough time for this *every day,* but they found with a little "tweaking" and creative partnership, they were able to do it without neglecting other areas of their lives.

The third step is to **enjoy life in the present**: live the present moment according to your schedule. First you decided how to improve your life (your personal goals), then you decided when to do it (your schedule), and now you can focus on living the present moment according to your schedule. Do what belongs to each moment as if you were born to do only that, without regrets about what you have not done in the past and without worrying about what you still have to do in the future. Focus on each activity as something special because you are giving your life to it, and that moment will never exist again.

Cindy, a successful executive, gave seminars on time management. She carried her virtual office with her while traveling cross-country on business. She took pride in her efficiency, but her marriage and her health were paying a high price for it. Her husband had serious doubts about the future of their marriage and she kept increasing and switching medications to be able to perform at the level expected from her at work. Her life felt like a runaway train about to derail. She feared destroying what she valued most. She needed to shift from a task management mode to a time management mode. She re-evaluated the seven rooms of her house and acknowledged that the only one that looked good was her job. The rest of the house needed care and investment. She answered the four questions that we have described in the previous pages and developed a new vision, motivation, strategy, and time commitment for each room. The last question about time commitment translated into a single sheet of paper that defined clearly where she was going to invest her time each week, and the best tasks for that time period. She has begun to experience a new vision and rhythm in her life, and is learning to stop time by living in the present without contaminating it with actions that do not belong in that moment. Her marriage and her health already have shown the benefits.

6.   Mental Fitness

Mental fitness is the ability to focus your mind on what is important and to remove "toxic" thoughts. An unfocused mind often reacts to what happens instead of acting on how you want to live. You end up spending increasing amounts of time in crisis management, letting what seems urgent stop you from doing what is truly important.

Your mind is constantly visited by uninvited thoughts that alter how you feel about other people and yourself. Such toxic thoughts distort your interpretation of reality, provoking negative feelings and behaviors. How you think determines how you feel and what you do.

Toxic thoughts are so prevalent that we need to develop mental "antidotes" by which we replace them as quickly as possible with positive thoughts. This does not mean pronouncing positive affirmations to ourselves, but rather focusing our minds on what we want and value.

The Toxic Thinking Inventory describes ten of the most common toxic thoughts. Completing it will help make you aware of how often you dwell on them. Afterwards, we will supply the antidotes. When you realize that you are having a toxic thought, act as if you had picked up a burning coal. As soon as you are aware of it, drop it and replace it with its antidote. You may need to practice this exercise hundreds of times each day. Some of our clients have laminated "Antidotes for Toxic Thinking" and keep it handy for easy reference. The more you practice, the better you become at it, and the greater the mental freedom that you will enjoy. You improve your mental fitness every time you replace a toxic thought with its antidote.

TOXIC THINKING INVENTORY

Circle the answer that best describes how often you think in the following terms:

> 1 = Never
> 2 = A little
> 3 = Sometimes
> 4 = Pretty much
> 5 = A lot

1) I pay more attention to the negative than the positive. 1 2 3 4 5

2) I think in "all-or-nothing," "always or never" terms. 1 2 3 4 5

3) I make decisions based on how I feel. 1 2 3 4 5

4) I think of others in critical ways. 1 2 3 4 5

5) I worry about the future and all that can go wrong. 1 2 3 4 5

6) I blow things out of proportion. 1 2 3 4 5

7) I feel helpless, unable to make choices. 1 2 3 4 5

8) I assume people's motives. 1 2 3 4 5

9) I stereotype people that I do not know well. 1 2 3 4 5

10) I place finishing tasks before relating well with others 1 2 3 4 5

ANTIDOTES TO TOXIC THINKING

Toxic Thought	Antidote
Negative Bias (Focusing only on the negative)	**Focus on the existing positive**
All or Nothing (Thinking in extreme, rigid and global terms)	**Think about specific ways to improve gradually**
Emotional Reasoning (Interpretations or decisions based on feelings)	**Make decisions based on your values**
Criticizing/Blaming (Judging others)	**Adjust your expectations, assume responsibility, and practice assertiveness**
Worrying (Living in fear of the future)	**Discern what depends on you, decide when you are going to do it and live the present moment**
Dramatizing (Blowing things out of proportion)	**Assess the importance of an event according to your values**
Helplessness (Thinking that you have no choices)	**Choose your thoughts, goals, expectations, and way of treating others**
Assuming (Guessing other people's motives)	**Ask people about their motives**
Labeling (Stereotyping people negatively)	**Label behaviors not persons**
Legalizing (Rule-oriented vs. person-oriented)	**First take care of the person, then take care of the task**

Let's take a closer look at these toxic thoughts, so you become better at replacing them as quickly as possible. If you fail, you need not get discouraged. You may have missed an opportunity, but you can start again and become better at it. We will describe each toxic thought in detail, as well as its antidote. You may wish to write some of your own toxic thoughts under the examples provided and practice replacing them with the antidote.

Negative Bias

You reveal a negative bias whenever your mind pays selective attention towards the negative within you, other people, or outside events. Every person or event has positive and negative elements, but a negative bias makes you focus only on the negative, distorting reality.

Dwelling on the negative is like wearing dark glasses that make you see the dark side in everything, discounting the positive. This type of toxic thinking can lead you to spend an incredible amount of time, energy, and resources trying to eliminate the negative believing that it will bring you happiness. In reality, *happiness is not found in decreasing the negative but in increasing the positive.*

Antidote for Negative Bias
Focus on the positive that exists in the person
or situation.

Example:
Toxic thought: "She is so critical!"
Antidote: "She is also honest, loyal and generous."

All or Nothing

You engage in all or nothing thinking when you think in rigid or extreme terms, see life as black or white, or use words such as "always" or "never." Few things in life happen this way. Most events and behaviors have multiple causes. Discern how to increase or decrease the probability that a certain outcome might follow.

Antidote for "All or Nothing"
Consider specific ways to improve
the situation gradually.

Example:

Toxic thought: "He never pays attention to my needs."

Antidote: "I will ask him to set aside 30 minutes in the evening for us to share our day."

Jim suffered from depression. He thought that everything about his life was terrible, that it would never get better, and that he was to blame. He thought that negative events had ruined every aspect of his life permanently, and blamed himself. Fortunately he learned to replace these toxic thoughts with their antidotes. He learned to look at his life in specific instead of global ways and started to take small steps in the right direction to activate meaningful changes. He was feeling overwhelmed and helpless about the changes needed to improve his life until he decided to implement one small change at a time that was within his reach. He eventually realized that what he called personal failures were actually moments of adversity, some caused by factors beyond his control. Once he discerned those areas over which he had control and began acting on them, his feelings of helplessness dissipated.

Emotional Reasoning

Emotional reasoning causes you to make a decision primarily according to how you feel. Feelings are important, but as we have discussed in chapter 1, they are unstable and influenced by many factors not under your immediate control. A solid decision is based on your values. Core values, consistent across circumstances and time, reflect your core identity. Experience has probably shown that whenever you made a decision based on your core values, you felt good about it. After all, what truly defines you are the values that motivate your actions.

Antidote for "Emotional Reasoning"
Make decisions based on your values.

Example:

Toxic thought: "I feel inadequate; therefore I can do nothing to help."

Antidote: "I value cooperation; therefore I will offer my help."

Terri had difficulty forgiving Mike for the way he treated her parents at a family gathering. She withdrew emotionally and was waiting for her feelings of resentment to disappear before she tried to communicate with him as they used to. The more she waited for her feelings to go away, the more she ruminated over the incident and the worse she felt towards him. Eventually she realized the toxicity of her approach. Because she valued their relationship, she decided to initiate meaningful communication and activate a process of forgiveness. She expressed her feelings and Mike gave her the apology that she needed. Making decisions according to her values did not mean ignoring her feelings; on the contrary they were understood and honored.

Criticizing and Blaming

We refer here to non-constructive criticism, as when you judge your partner without love. It is easy to blame your partner for a negative event, instead of trying to understand the multiple factors that might have caused or contributed to it. This type of criticism is one of the most destructive forces in a marriage, because it creates a spirit of division. It can lead one partner to justify his or her decision to stop loving, and the relationship begins to deteriorate.

To make this antidote work, start by adjusting your expectations about your partner. Make sure that you have accepted your partner's current level of functioning and that your expectations are realistic. For example, if your partner rarely plays with the kids during the week, it would be realistic to ask him or her to spend half an hour on some nights until it gradually becomes a daily event.

An antidote for blaming is taking responsibility for how you may have contributed to a mutual problem. This is not always obvious because your contribution might not be something negative that you did but something positive that you failed to do. If you cannot think of anything that you could have done to prevent or reduce the problem, ask your partner; in most cases, he or she will tell you.

Criticism is an attempt to stop your partner from doing something that you do not want him or her to do. A more effective approach is to communicate what you want by using assertiveness. We will elaborate on practicing assertiveness in chapter 9. A simple strategy is to stop before you say something critical and ask yourself: "What do I want him or her to do?" Once you know the answer, communicate your request as a respectful invitation.

Antidotes for "Criticizing and Blaming"
Have realistic expectations, assume responsibility
for your contribution to the problem,
and practice assertiveness.

Example:
Toxic thought: "You are such a slob!"
Antidote: "I would appreciate it if you would clean this room today."

Worrying

Worry lets your fears for the future contaminate the present. Sometimes you need to plan the future, but worrying is more than mere planning. When you worry you try to control the future by thinking about everything that could go wrong in a futile attempt to control things that lie beyond your influence.

Worries steal the present. They take your attention away from what you should be thinking about in that moment. The useless waste of energy spent worrying about something out of your control resembles a passenger who keeps walking toward the front of the airplane as a way to get to the destination faster.

You might think that you can control the future through obsessive thinking or compulsive rituals. However, you overestimate your control over the future, and your failure to control those events further feeds your anxiety. Whenever you feel concerned about something, discern first *what* about that issue depends on you, then decide *when* you are going to do your part, concentrating on doing what you are supposed to do in that present moment and entrusting all the rest to God with renewed confidence in his care for you and your loved ones. If your anxiety prevents you from fulfilling your basic responsibilities, seek professional help.

Antidotes for Worrying
Discern what depends on you, decide when you
are going to act on it, and focus on
living the present moment.

Example:

Toxic thought: "I worry about my health."

Antidote: "I am going to eat healthier foods and exercise daily at 7:00 AM. Now I will focus on playing with the kids."

Dramatizing

You are dramatizing when you blow things out of proportion or over-react to events. Determine the importance of an event according to objective criteria or values. Otherwise you might spend your time in crisis management, addressing what you think is urgent but forgetting to address what is important. It is like missing the forest for the trees.

Patients with life-threatening illnesses have taught us to put things in proper perspective. One wise patient said, "I always ask myself, what is the eternal significance of this event?"

Antidote for Dramatizing
Assess the importance of an event
according to your values.

Example:

Toxic thought: "We argue so much. Maybe our marriage is doomed."

Antidote: "Most couples have rough moments. We can seek professional help and learn better conflict-resolution skills."

Carol worried about Steve's emotional detachment and lack of interest in her. She complained that he spent most of his time lost in his own thoughts and rarely shared his thoughts with her. She interpreted his avoidance as an indication that he was unhappy with their marriage and began to prepare herself emotionally for a divorce. Steve saw their marriage in quite a different light. He acknowledged his introversion and his difficulty articulating his own feelings or showing interest in Carol's, but he was willing to work on it. He also disclosed to us a concern over his company's downsizing but did not want to burden Carol with it. Carol realized that both of them valued their marriage and were committed to it, but they needed to develop better communication. They began to set aside thirty minutes each night to talk with each other. He is still reserved but no longer detached.

Helplessness

You are thinking with helplessness when you relinquish your ability to make changes or decisions. You might let past negative experiences convince you that no matter what you do nothing is going to change or that your actions will not make a difference. Do not let past negative experiences prevent you from making good choices in the present.

When you think and act as if you are helpless, you distort reality because you assume that everything will always go wrong and that it is going to be your fault. In reality things sometimes might go wrong due to factors beyond your control. However, you do have control over many aspects of your life. You can set your own goals, and can determine for yourself how you interpret the events of your life, what you expect of others, and how you respond to others, even those who may not have treated you well.

All of us experience moments of sadness or depression, generally due to painful events such as the loss of a dear person or a valued possession. These feelings are appropriate and we eventually overcome them by using our own coping skills, the support available to us, or both. If you experience levels of depression that leave you unable to fulfill your basic responsibilities, seek help from a mental health professional.

Antidote for Helplessness
Choose your interpretations, your expectations, your goals, and your ways of treating other people.

Example:

Toxic thought: "There is nothing I can do to improve our marriage."

Antidote: "I can give my spouse more attention, affection, and appreciation every day."

Assuming

You are assuming when you think that you can read other peoples' minds or when you jump to conclusions about their motives. This type of toxic thinking can cause severe damage in a marriage. When you assume the wrong motives for your partner's behavior you are questioning his or her integrity and risking character assassination. Assuming the motives behind another's actions can cause emotional damage, mistrust, and loss of respect. It may block any process to resolve a conflict.

Whenever you want to know why your spouse has behaved in certain ways, ask him or her in a direct, respectful, non-accusatory manner, with a genuine desire to understand, not to condemn your partner or use his or her motives as a reason to attack.

Antidote for Assuming
Ask others about their motives.

Example:
Toxic thought: "She is trying to make me pay for what I did yesterday."
Antidote: "I would like to know what motivated you to do that."

Ben decided to stop talking to Sheryl for several days when she failed to do something that he asked her. He said, "She wanted to hurt me! If she cared about me she would have done what I asked her." Eventually Ben asked her about it and she replied: "I didn't understand that it was that important to you. I didn't forget on purpose, to hurt you. I had other things on my mind." He is now more willing to ask Sheryl before he assumes her intentions.

Labeling

You are labeling when you categorize people according to negative stereotypes. This type of toxic thinking makes you generalize from the negative behaviors of some people, reducing your total vision of them to those labels. When labeling becomes extreme it can turn into prejudice based on race, religion, gender, age, political views, socioeconomic status, or cultural background.

You engage in labeling whenever you define your partner using offensive adjectives or nicknames intended to shame. At times your partner will do negative things. In those instances, define that behavior in negative terms, not the person.

Avoiding labeling is particularly important in marriages in which the partners come from different ethnic, religious, or socio-cultural backgrounds.

Antidote for Labeling
Label the behavior, not the person.

Example:

Toxic thought: "You are so lazy!"

Antidote: "When you procrastinate, I have a big problem with you."

Rosa complained that Walter cared more about his job than his family. Walter defended himself by saying that she had unrealistic expectations that he would act like a Latino man and that she should accept his German upbringing. They kept labeling each other according to cultural stereotypes and they lost sight of each other as persons. Gradually they stopped using labels as weapons and began discussing behavioral expectations in respectful and personal ways. They transformed their cultural diversity into an asset by appreciating their differences and by learning to behave towards each other more sensitively.

Legalizing

You are legalizing when you reduce life to a series of rules and responsibilities. This type of toxic thinking makes you look at life in legalistic terms. After a few years, some marriages look more like a contract than a covenant. When you get trapped into legalistic thinking you might find yourself frequently using words such as: should, must, ought, or have to. Responsibilities and expectations are necessary in any marriage, but they are the means to an end. The end is to love one another. Spouses who look at their relationship as a division of labor or as a means for completing tasks efficiently will find their marriage going backwards.

When partners define a marriage as a list of rules and responsibilities, true love languishes and family life becomes an emotional prison. We need to rediscover "the spirit of the law" and remind ourselves that people are more important than tasks, and that tasks are at the service of people. The value of any task depends upon the love with which it is carried out.

Antidote for Legalizing
First take care of your partner,
and then take care of the task.

Example:

Toxic thought: "First let's finish the project, and then we will talk."

Antidote: "Is there anything that you need before we start the project?"

Freedom from Unrealistic Expectations

Mental fitness requires eliminating not only toxic thoughts but also unrealistic expectations. Are your expectations of others based on reality? If not, you are a prime candidate for self-inflicted disappointment, anger, resentment, stress, and unhappiness. It is a common misperception that having realistic expectations means having to lower expectations or standards and settle for mediocrity or stagnation. Some people are afraid to accept others as they are for fear that they will never change and they will interpret acceptance as approval. In fact, you can accept people's current level of maturity yet at the same time disapprove of some of their actions or disagree with some of their words.

Here are some examples of unrealistic expectations. See if you recognize any in yourself.

I Should Get Rid of "Difficult" People in My Life

We are not talking here about your spouse but about those people that make life difficult. Given current estimates of the frequency in the general population of people with psychological problems, levels of stress, family dysfunction, and health disorders, at least 25% of the people that you meet during the day are going to be "difficult." Sooner or later, you too may be a difficult person for someone else.

It is realistic to expect one out of four people you meet to be difficult. Difficult people cannot be eliminated or avoided. Learn to cope with them. In chapters 9, 10, and 11 we will offer strategies for coping with them.

I Should Be Able to Change My Spouse

This unrealistic expectation hits closer to home. This is one of the most common hidden agendas of people in difficult marriages. They think that they will be happy if they can succeed in changing some negative behavior in their partner. After years of unsuccessful attempts, some seek professional help thinking, "If I cannot change my spouse, perhaps the therapist will." Many a time, one partner has dragged the other to therapy with the hidden and unrealistic expectation that the therapist would change a spouse against his or her will. Sometimes they are candid or desperate enough to acknowledge such a motive. One husband, while his wife was in another room, whispered to John, "I will pay you anything if you change her!" Since he had a seven-figure salary, the proposition was enticing; but knowing better, John asked him: "How much are you willing to pay if you change?" The client looked puzzled and replied, "I am not the one with the problem here. I cannot think of anything that I need to change." John responded, "Why don't we ask her?" When she returned John told her, "Your husband would like to know if there is anything that he can change about himself that will help the marriage." Before John finished his sentence she pulled a list from her purse that she had written the night before but had not yet shown him. Eventually, they selected a couple of behaviors that he acknowledged that he could improve. She also listened to her husband's suggestions for improvement. Once they stopped trying to change each other and out of love for each other started changing themselves, they made progress.

Your partner will change when your partner decides to change. However, you can increase the probability that he or she will change by modeling your willingness to change out of love for him or her.

I Should Be a Perfect Mate

Unrealistic expectations about yourself might make you think that your love should be perfect and constant. It is realistic, however, to accept yourself with your imperfections and limitations, willing to start again whenever you fail. Mastering the art of loving your partner will take a lifetime. You must redefine "perfection" as "continuous improvement."

Whenever you fail to love your partner as you planned, do not dwell on your failure. Instead, start over with greater humility and determination. Expect failure as a necessary part of success when you define success not in all or nothing terms but as gradual improvement. Every time that you start again you become stronger and more resilient. Thinking that you should never fail is actually delusional and arrogant. A failure to love your partner is best viewed as a missed opportunity. Recognize that in the present you have a brand new opportunity to love.

Picture marriage as a home that you are building day by day. On those days that you failed to love, you stopped building it. Once you decide to love again, you need not rebuild the whole house from scratch; you continue where you left off. Whatever you have built already out of love cannot be destroyed or taken away by a failure to love. The more you practice starting again, the more agile you become, and the more quickly you learn to start again.

One of the differences between spiritually immature and mature people is that the immature are easily discouraged by their own failures and ruminate on them, whereas when mature people experience personal failure they start again much faster and turn their thoughts to others instead of to themselves.

These examples of *realistic* expectations illustrate some basic truths about human behavior:

The Positive and the Negative Co-exist in Every Human Being

You should expect to encounter both in every person, including your spouse and yourself.

The Value of the Positive Outweighs the Negative

A pound of gold is not the same as a pound of dirt. Look for the gold in your spouse and expect to find it.

The Negative Does Not Erase the Positive

Any positive action done out of love remains forever. Expect to build on the solid foundation of the positive that is already there.

The Positive Displaces the Negative

An act of love can actually fill the void left by its lack. Instead of trying to remove the negative, focus on promoting the positive and expect to see the negative decrease.

In chapter 12 we discuss the "divine alchemy" that can transform any negative into a positive.

7. De-Stressing Your Life

Before reading further, take a moment to complete the following Stress Management Questionnaire.

STRESS MANAGEMENT QUESTIONNAIRE

Circle the number which best describes how often you use the following stress reduction approaches:

$$1 = Never$$
$$2 = A\ little$$
$$3 = Sometimes$$
$$4 = Pretty\ much$$
$$5 = A\ lot$$

1) I eat healthy food, including fruits
   and vegetables, every day   1 2 3 4 5

2) I drink 8 glasses of water daily   1 2 3 4 5

3) I sleep 7 to 8 hours each night   1 2 3 4 5

4) I practice 30 minutes of planned
   physical exercise daily   1 2 3 4 5

5) I practice deep breathing exercises daily   1 2 3 4 5

6) I practice relaxation techniques daily   1 2 3 4 5

7) I engage in some recreational activity
   at least once a week   1 2 3 4 5

8) I replace toxic thoughts with healthy
   ones within minutes   1 2 3 4 5

9) I have realistic expectations about
   others and myself   1 2 3 4 5

10) I have short-term goals in all areas
   of my life   1 2 3 4 5

11) I follow a weekly schedule with time
    for all areas of my life   1 2 3 4 5

12) I live in the present without worrying
    about the future   1 2 3 4 5

13) I live a simple life within my budget   1 2 3 4 5

14) I keep my work & home environment
    organized, without clutter   1 2 3 4 5

15) I spend time weekly strengthening or
    increasing my friendships   1 2 3 4 5

16) I use effective communication skills   1 2 3 4 5

17) I find "win-win" solutions to conflicts
    with others   1 2 3 4 5

18) I tell others how I want to be treated
    without complaining   1 2 3 4 5

19) If criticized, I focus on the other
    person's expectations   1 2 3 4 5

20) I practice 30 minutes of daily
    meditation   1 2 3 4 5

21) I have a clear meaning and purpose
    in my life   1 2 3 4 5

22) I am able to forgive and initiate
    reconciliation with others   1 2 3 4 5

23) I live a spirituality that helps me
    overcome suffering   1 2 3 4 5

Pay special attention to any item you scored 3 or below. Most of the stress management strategies that relate to a particular item are self-explanatory or are described in various sections of this book.

Your life will always contain some stress because it is part of coping with physical, psychological, social, and spiritual changes or challenges. Your overall health depends on your ability to manage it, eliminate self-induced stress, and develop a healthy and balanced lifestyle. The strategies that you need to implement encompass your whole person: body, thoughts, lifestyle, emotions, relationships, and soul.

A major source of stress for all people in contemporary society, including couples, is the culture of excess. To counteract it, we need to exercise the constant, voluntary choice to simplify our lives. Simplicity is not about deprivation or austerity. It's about freedom from clutter and unhealthy habits; enjoying what we have instead of desiring more; caring for others and for our common environment. The secret to simple living lies in four maxims:

- Donate to charity what you do not use or need.

- Buy only what you need and can afford.

- Share what you have with others.

- Live a lifestyle that shows respect for the earth.

Give to Charity What You Do Not Use or Need

Weekly or monthly, de-clutter your home, garage, closets, pantry, or drawers of anything that you have not used for months or that you no longer need. Give those things that are still useful to charity.

One day, John came home from work and found the driveway filled with various household objects. At first, he felt pleased that Claire had undertaken spring cleaning. When he asked what she intended to do with all the items, she stated in a matter-of-fact voice, "We are giving them to the poor." John's surprise turned into uneasy questioning: "What do you mean? Those things in the driveway happen to be my stuff! Since when do you make a unilateral decision about my things?" Claire argued that he had not used any of those things for at least a year. He replied: "Yes, but you never know when I might need them again!" The discussion went back and forth until John felt a slight tug on his pants. Their six-year-old son, Paul, was trying to get his attention. When John looked at him, he stated, "Dad, you always talk about sharing with the poor; well, this is your chance!" The simplicity and truthfulness of Paul's statement disarmed him. The next day a truck from Saint Vincent de Paul took everything—tools, books, appliances, furniture, and electronic equipment. Years have passed and we cannot think of a single day when we missed any of it.

Of all the things we own, 25% are superfluous. Most of us wear fewer than 50% of the clothes that we have in our closets. Survey your house, and put aside everything that you are not using but still in working condition, all your duplicates, all the things that you no longer need, and give all of it to a suitable charity. We try to do this each month.

Buy Only What You Need and Can Afford

Decide to live within your means, or even better, just below your means. Establish a monthly budget. During the year 2000, consumers spent 24% of their income on necessities, 56% on upgrading possessions they already owned, and 20% on luxuries. Most people make a weekly trip to the shopping mall without intending to buy any specific item. On average, Americans spend six hours each week shopping, but only one with their families. Go to the mall when you need to buy something, and avoid the temptation to buy sale items that you do not really need. Resist using shopping as a form of entertainment or relaxation.

Share What You Have

Develop a culture of mutual sharing to counteract our dominant culture of private consumption. Make an effort to get to know your neighbors and your community. Offer them any of your resources, possessions, or personal talents and interests that could help them.

Assess how to share such possessions as tools, books, toys, home and garden implements, educational materials, or automobiles with others. We like to look around our house and ask, "Who else could use this?" We do not necessarily give the item away, but we do offer it to other people who can use it. Friends of ours have created a "tool co-op" among neighborhood families who share their garden and household tools.

Your most precious possession is your time. With whom could you share it besides your family? In the last decade, the average time dedicated to hospitality has decreased from six hours a month to one. How much time do you dedicate to hospitality every month? We know people who have created a "babysitting co-op" to allow parents time to spend together as couples. Other people have created an "elderly co-op" to allow adults caring for their parents to have time as a couple or as a family.

You could share your knowledge through teaching, tutoring or mentoring those who cannot afford to pay. It could be as simple as teaching a family member home repairs or as demanding as mentoring an unemployed person seeking a job. Think about who could benefit from what you know.

Finally, share with people interested in learning more about spiritual life. You could teach catechism, Sunday school, Bible study, or participate in a small faith-sharing group.

Live a Lifestyle That Shows Respect for the Earth

We are all interdependent. Our planet's resources belong to all of us. Whenever you can, eliminate pollution and waste and conserve energy. You can make a difference by changing your own lifestyle.

8. The Soul of Autonomy

Often we measure our self-worth by our accomplishments, especially in a culture that defines people in terms of what they do. What we do should express who we are, not the other way around.

Self-worth grows from the soul, the compass of your life, your source of meaning and purpose. Your soul is the source of spiritual power that transcends you and connects you with others.

The soul of autonomy, its spiritual center, is the presence of Jesus within you: "The life I live now is not my own; it is Christ living in me" (Galatians 2:20). How can Jesus' presence increase in you so that you become more like him? You must come to define yourself as Jesus did, and he defined himself as the way, the truth, and the life.

The Way: Living God's Will in the Present Moment

Jesus is the way to the Father. We become more like him when we live the Father's will moment by moment. To do the will of God does not mean to follow a set of rules, but to establish a partnership with God, allowing him to show us our journey, day by day, moment by moment. It requires complete confidence that everything he wants or allows to happen can lead us to a greater union with him.

When a friend of ours asked Mother Teresa of Calcutta to explain the will of God, she told him, "The will of God is not something that you do, but something that you are." To us, that answer suggests that God is love and wants us to be love like him. We can do many things out of love for God, but he is primarily interested in us *being love* like him. When he came to face the possibility of his own imminent death, John came to understand, in a dramatic and real way, that at the end of our lives the only thing that matters to God is how much we have loved.

One day, many years ago, I was climbing in the Pyrenees alone. I lost my footing and found myself hanging by my fingertips at 12,000 feet! My precarious grasp would not hold me for long. In horror I anticipated a free fall of over a thousand feet against the rocks below. Knowing that I would fall to my death, I searched anxiously for the meaning of my life, and I saw in a flash all of its highlights. The voice of God within me interrupted my thoughts about my academic and professional achievements. "These accomplishments are not your life. Your real life is whatever you lived out of love for me and for others; all the rest doesn't matter to me." I felt devastated that I had spent my short life in an empty, insignificant search for success. I asked God to forgive me for failing to do the only thing that mattered to him. Soon afterwards, as I fell, I felt the embrace of God's gentleness and infinite compassion. My plunge ended in a huge thorn bush that I had not noticed before. I picked myself out and descended safely to the bottom of the mountain where some friends were waiting for me. They were shocked to see me bleeding from the scratches of the thorns, yet amazed that my face was radiant with joy. When I explained what had just happened, they exclaimed, "You must be happy because you escaped death miraculously!" I told them, "No. I am happy because I have discovered the meaning of life! The secret of happiness is to do everything out of love." Since that moment, I recall at the end of each day that what will remain at the end of my life is not how much I have accomplished, but how much I have loved.

Jesus summed up the will of God in the two great commandments: love God with your whole heart, soul, and mind; and love your neighbor as yourself (Matthew 22:37). He also gave us another new commandment, one that he called "his": "This is my commandment: love one another as I have loved you" (John 15:12). We can be certain that we are doing the will of God when we live these commandments.

In chapter 5 we presented the seven rooms of the house of self. God wants you to take care of this "house" that he has entrusted to you. You need to discern how much time

God wants you to allocate to each room each week. *Time* is God's gift of life to us. It is not our time; it is his, and we are to administer it well. From this perspective, there is always enough time for doing God's will. For example, God certainly wants us to work as long as we are able—but how many hours a week? The same applies to time for family, spiritual life, friends, health, education, and the community. Our own weekly master calendar allocates time to each of the seven rooms, so as to remind ourselves at any given moment where God wants us to be. When we move into a new "time zone," we identify the most important task in that moment. Finally, whatever we do, we do it for no other reason but love. When we plan our lives like this, we experience God's presence within us. Regularly, we review, coordinate and adjust our weekly schedule to balance it according to what we agree together is God's will for us.

When you live the will of God in the present moment out of love, Jesus lives in you. This approach brings a hectic and fragmented life into focus, one that gives glory to God and joy to others. The purpose of a balanced lifestyle is not to feel comfortable but to transform your life into the masterpiece that God intended when he created you. To do so, place your past in God's mercy, place your future in God's providence, and root yourself in God's will in the present moment.

Try This

Create a weekly master schedule
discerning how much time God wants you
to allocate to each room of your house of self.
Then, live God's will in the present
according to your schedule

The Truth: Incarnating the Word of God

The truth is not a concept, but a person: Jesus, the Word of the Father. Your life is truthful when you listen to his words, live them, and share its fruit with others.

Listening to the Word

God created you with a unique design of love. One of the best ways to discover that design starts by listening to his voice, usually during daily meditation. Most people do not seem to understand what meditation is, or how to put aside time for it. Meditation is an intimate and loving conversation with God, where we let him do most of the talking.

We have found how important it is to start each day meditating. Each of us meditates by ourselves for 30 minutes. During that time we listen to what God wants for us that day. We start the meditation by placing ourselves in front of God, emptying from our minds any worries, memories, fantasies or unrelated thoughts; from our will any desires; from our heart any attachments to any person. We focus our total attention on God's loving presence, silencing everything within us and around us so as to become totally attentive.

When we feel ready to listen, we open the Holy Scriptures or an inspirational book and read slowly. As soon as a particular word or phrase touches our soul, we stop reading and begin to dialogue with God, listening to his suggestions on how to put it into practice. We conclude the meditation with a practical resolution for the day based on the main message that we received during the meditation. We usually write it down in our daily planner as a reminder of how to live the day. We have meditated on the Scriptures for years, yet every time we discover some new pearl of wisdom that offers light and strength for our daily journey. For us, meditation is an endless discovery of God's personal love and it helps us to understand how to love God and others.

Living the Word

Throughout the day we apply the practical resolution from our meditation, trying to "incarnate" God's words by thinking, feeling, and acting as Jesus would in our place. Listening to God's words is like planting a seed. Living them is allowing the seed to grow and bear fruit. The only way to understand the meaning of Jesus' words is to live them. Insight into his words is only the beginning; when we become those words, we discover new life: Jesus living in us.

Sharing the Fruit

Later, at an opportune moment, we share the experiences of putting God's words into practice with those who share our faith or want to know about it. Experiences that we do not share can wither and lose their meaning. Those shared out of love can transform the person receiving them. We feel joy when people who have attended one of our presentations thank us for the positive impact we have had on their lives. Often, they mention that what transformed their lives were not so much the ideas we presented but the experiences we shared. We believe that those experiences manifest God working in our lives. It is that divine presence, not us who has touched them.

Try This

Set aside 30 minutes each day for meditation.
Listen to God's message, live it throughout the day,
and share the fruit with others.

The Life: the Art of Christian Loving

Jesus' presence within us transforms our lives and our relationships. He teaches us to love in a different way. His way of loving has distinctive characteristics; here we are going to reflect on four of them: He took the initiative in loving, loved everybody, loved concretely, and loved to the end. We, too, can love the same way that Jesus did. "The love of God has been poured into our hearts through the Holy Spirit that has been given to us" (Romans 5:5).

Take the Initiative to Love

"We love, because he first loved us" (1 John 4:19).

We manifest our dignity and freedom as children of God when we take the initiative to love others unconditionally.

Taking the initiative to love your partner and each other person that you meet creates the best conditions for mutuality. Every time you decide to be the first to love you experience the freedom and the joy of unconditional giving.

Love Every Person

"He died for all so that those who live might live no longer for themselves, but for him who for their sakes died and was raised up" (2 Corinthians 5:15).

Jesus loved and died for everybody, including his enemies. Christian love transcends the limits we place on our relationships because of personal preferences or past hurts.

Claire experienced this dimension of Christian love vividly when she studied in Israel.

> I was walking from the corner market when I heard a commotion. In front of me a Jewish student and an Arab boy had begun arguing, and soon a group of other students and local villagers gathered, yelling and throwing rocks at each other. Witnessing such events that year changed my life. Our experiences led me and my fellow students to consider how we could bring tangible evidence of God's love to everyone despite the hate and fear we saw. Living God's love meant loving each one we met, regardless of race, religion, or political persuasion. We put love where there was no love, and we saw and experienced many moments of healing. This time, more than any other, made me realize that God's will was to love each person I met.

The more you practice loving the different people that you encounter throughout the day, the more your ability to love your partner increases. The unique needs of each person that you meet prompt you to increase your capacity to love. By the time you get home in the evening, you will be even more capable of loving your partner and your family. Not loving each person you meet throughout the day will diminish the energy, flexibility, and endurance you need to face the challenges waiting for you at home.

When we decide to love the person who happens to be next to us something new happens to our life. We allow God to intervene in our lives in unexpected ways. He shows us the direction that he wants us to follow.

Love Concretely

"The son of Man has come not to be served by others, but to serve, to give his own life as a ransom for the many" (Matthew 20:28).

Jesus demonstrated his love with concrete actions aimed at serving others.

Your love for your partner is real when it becomes concrete and visible. In chapter 4 we described how the final stage of empathy is always a concrete behavior aimed at benefiting your partner. Most couples need to increase the frequency of these acts of intelligent love. You might think that home is a place to rest after a hard day at work. You should find time to rest, but not from loving. Whenever you practice acts of empathy they will energize and refresh you. Often, you will receive them back in return.

Love to the End

"There is no greater love than this: to lay down one's life for one's friends" (John 15:13).

Jesus freely gave his life for us. His love reveals the intensity and duration that ours should have. How far are you willing to go to show your love for your partner? During the last few minutes of our commute home from work, we ready ourselves to encounter each other and our son. Before we enter the house, we ask ourselves this question: "Am I ready to lay down my life for them?" Once we make that decision, we can manage whatever we encounter inside. Any demand made of us is less than what we are willing to give. It is like signing a blank check and letting the other person write the amount. As long as we are ready to give our lives for each other no one can overdraw our account.

Within the soul of autonomy, the spiritual connects with the psychological. Living the will of God in the present moment balances all the areas of your life; living the Word of God frees your mind from toxic thoughts; living the Christian art of loving, makes your life a gift to others.

Try This

*Practice one characteristic of Christian love
each week of the month:*

During the first week
I will take the initiative to love.

During the second week
I will love each person that I meet.

During the third week
I will love concretely.

During the fourth week
I will love to the end.

Part 3

*M*utuality: the Joy of Unity

Marriage requires not only empathy and autonomy, but also mutuality, which itself has three components: communication, conflict resolution, and the healing power of forgiveness and reconciliation. Marriage requires the integration of the "You" and the "I" into a creative "We." These three dimensions do not stand alone as self-contained units, but interact. When there is no empathy, the "You" is missing , and without the "You," a relationship cannot become a "We." When one partner lacks autonomy, the relationship is lacking an "I." Mutuality requires the integration of "You" and "I" into the transcendent interdependence of "We."

Often, people with low empathy skills (highly independent and with narcissistic tendencies) attract people with low autonomy skills (codependent and insecure). Such a couple presents the illusion of a good relationship because the codependent partner generally avoids conflict at all costs. However, once the insecure partner gains self-confidence and greater autonomy, he or she usually initiates separation from their self-centered mate. Healthy marriages pay simultaneous attention to the "You," "I," and "We" dimensions.

9. The Art of Communication

A marriage strengthens every time partners communicate authentically. Communication is not reserved for special moments. It is not like the icing on a cake, it is the cake! How can you become truly one without sharing your life and your soul with each other? Poor communication creates unnecessary conflicts and turns a marriage into an endless series of conflicts to be solved or an unfulfilling distribution of roles and responsibilities.

The art of communication includes sharing, listening, and feedback. It promotes mutual understanding and appreciation, leading to one of the aspects of a fulfilled Christian marriage — unity in diversity. Communicating with your partner should be enjoyable. Unfortunately many couples reduce communication to problem solving. Partners often take "I want to talk with you" to mean "I have a problem with you and we need to talk." Communication and conflict resolution are different processes with different goals. Communication aims to increase mutual understanding and unity, whereas problem solving aims to resolve a conflict and promote behavioral change.

Partners should find time every day to communicate with one another about their lives. Communication usually has to do with sharing the past. It is important that partners agree to avoid conflict during these conversations. Unless there is an emergency, unresolved conflicts should wait for the one-hour weekly problem-solving session we discuss in chapter 10. In conflict resolution, which is future-oriented, partners reach consensus on new behaviors that are necessary to resolve a conflict.

The following questionnaire examines 13 key communication skills.

COMMUNICATION SKILLS QUESTIONNAIRE

Please circle the answer that best describes how often you use the following communication skills with your partner:

1 = Never
2 = A little
3 = Sometimes
4 = Pretty much
5 = A lot

1) Before I share, I see whether my
   partner is ready to listen.   1 2 3 4 5

2) I share meaningful personal experiences.   1 2 3 4 5

3) I share my feelings without venting.   1 2 3 4 5

4) I keep my sharing brief.   1 2 3 4 5

5) I listen with full attention and interest.   1 2 3 4 5

6) I listen respectfully, accepting my
   partner as he or she is.   1 2 3 4 5

7) I try to understand, without thinking
   about my answer.   1 2 3 4 5

8) I listen without interrupting.   1 2 3 4 5

9) I acknowledge what my partner
   has shared.   1 2 3 4 5

10) I validate what my partner has shared.   1 2 3 4 5

11) I give a positive response to what my
    partner has shared.   1 2 3 4 5

12) I ask relevant questions about what
    my partner has shared.   1 2 3 4 5

13) I feel that my partner understands me.   1 2 3 4 5

Now, let's take a closer look at each of these communication skills.

Before you share, see whether your partner
is ready to listen.

Timing can open the door to communication or close it. Communication should be spontaneous but not impulsive. Initiate at what seems an opportune moment or ask your partner when it would be good to talk. It helps to set aside a time that both find convenient for your daily sharing; do not schedule other activities during that time. Do not rush. Communication is like sharing a good meal. Hurrying it or forcing it will spoil the moment. If your partner cannot listen at the time that you would like, find another moment. If your partner never seems to have a good moment to listen, seek to discover the reason behind the delay or the avoidance.

Share meaningful thoughts, feelings,
and experiences.

Sometimes, partners fall into the habit of giving each other their personal "evening news," or talk about the people that they have encountered, but forget to share what it all meant. Real sharing communicates the meaning of an event or an encounter, or significant thoughts or feelings. Experienced partners probably know by heart most of the "news" about their lives at work or at home, but have no way of knowing what each day has meant unless they share it. The personal meaning of an event is the main course of the "meal" whereas the news about who, how, where and when are the side dishes. Partners could spend the whole day next to each other, see what each did that day and still not know what was most meaningful. *Deciding to share something meaningful means making a conscious decision to share yourself with your partner.*

Share your feelings without venting.

Before sharing, rehearse what you are going to say, so you share its meaning attractively. The "meal" that you are going to serve should be completely prepared and appetizing. For example, instead of venting the frustrations of the day when you get home use your commute time to reflect on the most significant events of the day and what they meant for you.

Feelings need to be shared, not "dumped" on each other. Some people think they can vent negative feelings so long as they use "I statements." Negative feelings can be shared without venting provided you also share a strategy to overcome them. For example, instead of saying only "I feel very worried about my job," you could say, "I feel very worried about my job and this is what I am going to do to about it ..." Sharing a raw, unappetizing meal with one another will hinder or prevent communication.

Be selective and share briefly.

Some people take the scenic route when they share and lose their partner's interest before reaching the conclusion. More is not always better. If you give people good food in small portions, they usually ask for more.

However if you serve more than they want, they will think twice before accepting another dinner invitation.

A reasonable goal is about 30 minutes a day in meaningful communication. If you find it hard to find the time, take it away from less vital activities such as watching TV or using the internet. Communication is a precious moment of emotional intimacy, far more valuable than the trivial activities with which we often fill our time.

Your own ability to listen can determine the quality of your partner's sharing. It is harder to listen than to talk. Next, we will examine how to become a great listener.

Give full attention and interest.

Think of listening as "EASY," an acronym that stands for Emptying yourself, Accepting your partner, Sensitivity, and Yielding. The first step in listening is to empty your own thoughts, feelings, or plans while your partner is talking to you. One of the best ways to empty yourself is to give your partner full attention and interest when he or she is talking. Emptying yourself, a form of self-denial, requires a conscious decision. The more you focus your attention and interest on your partner, the less you think about yourself and the more your partner will share. The amount of attention that you give conveys your partner's importance to you. If your partner wants to talk with you when you cannot give your full attention, let him or her know what time would be better.

Showing attention and interest in non-verbal ways, such as eye contact, posture, and facial expressions demonstrates an exquisite, radical love.

Accept what is shared, even if you disagree.

Acceptance is the second step in listening. Let your partner feel that you accept his or her difference from you and that you are willing to entertain different views, feelings, and experiences, without judgment, ridicule or rejection.

Some people complain that they feel emotionally vulnerable when they talk with their partners and so limit their sharing or avoid it altogether. They feel that they are on trial, and worry that everything they say could be used against them.

Facial expressions and posture need to reveal genuine openness and respect towards your partner. Effective sharing resembles preparing a healthy and attractive meal for your partner; effective listening resembles welcoming your partner to your home. Emptiness is the equivalent of opening the door and making room for your partner in your life. Acceptance is allowing your partner to feel at home with you. True acceptance means enjoying your partner just as he or she is.

Focus on understanding your partner,
not on preparing a response.

The third step in listening is to show sensitivity towards your partner. Once your partner feels at home, focus on understanding him or her. Unconditional acceptance is more than mere tolerance. It guarantees deep understanding because it reveals your willingness to learn something about your partner. This requires an attitude of wonder and genuine curiosity. The opposite is to believe that you already know all you need to know. If you activate your curiosity, listening becomes engaging and enjoyable.

It is tempting to prepare a response while your partner is still talking. This creates two simultaneous conversations: what your partner is telling you and the response that you are preparing. The second conversation, silent and internal, creates interference that prevents you from understanding what your partner is trying to tell you.

Listen without interrupting.

The final step in listening is yielding to your partner until he or she finishes talking. Interrupting your partner stops the communication process. You should interrupt only when you have another commitment that might keep you from listening any longer. In such a case, let your partner know when you can continue the conversation.

By showing your partner your personal attention, genuine acceptance, willingness to understand, and uninterrupted interest, she or he will share more freely and deeply. Remember EASY: Emptying yourself, Accepting your partner, Sensitivity, and Yielding.

Acknowledge what was shared.

Let your partner know whether you have understood through verbal feedback. In some couples, one partner will listen patiently but when the other has finished talking he or she asks, "Are you done?" then switch the conversation to themselves without acknowledging the gift that has been offered.

Provide feedback by acknowledging what your partner shared. You need not repeat what was said, but simply acknowledge in your own words the main content of what you heard. This will give your partner the opportunity to appreciate your understanding or, if that is not the case, to clarify what was shared. Your feedback can be a short sentence or an elaborate comment, depending on what your partner shared, but it should always convey your gratitude for his or her sharing.

Validate your spouse.

After you have acknowledged your partner's sharing, validate its content. *To validate means to value your partner's ideas, feelings and experiences even if you disagree with them.* It can be as simple as saying, "I am glad that you shared this with me because it helps me understand you better." It is a mistake to discount, trivialize or ridicule what was shared. Your partner needs to feel valued and affirmed.

Give a non-critical response.

If you want to give a specific comment, make sure that it comes across as an affirmation, not as a criticism. One common mistake is to give unsolicited advice that usually will annoy your partner and will shift the process from communication to problem solving. You can always share the positive impact that your partner's sharing had on you.

Ask relevant questions

What your partner shares may prompt questions or the desire to know more. The best questions are open ended, not ones that elicit a yes or no answer. A yes or no question such as "Did you feel upset?" will end the communication quickly. An open-ended question such as "Can you tell me more about what made you upset?" will encourage more sharing. The communication cycle is complete when both of you have had the opportunity to share, listen, give feedback, and feel valued and understood.

10. Solving Conflicts with Wisdom and Respect

Most conflicts between partners arise out of differences in the way they think, feel, or want to do things. The most common responses to a conflict are to fight, flee or freeze. When you fight you try to win the conflict and impose your ideas or your will on your partner. Some examples of a fight response are: blaming your partner for the conflict, criticizing your partner for his or her contribution to the conflict, shaming your partner for causing the conflict, ridiculing your partner's thoughts, feelings or behaviors, trivializing your partner's feelings or expectations or engaging in some form of verbal or physical abuse.

When you flee from a conflict, your fear and insecurity drive you to avoid the conflict. For example: withdrawing physically or emotionally, avoiding meaningful communication, isolating from your partner, giving your partner "the silent treatment" or making empty promises to get your partner off your back.

When you freeze in a conflict, your perception of the severity of the conflict makes you feel helpless and hopeless. For example: playing the victim or submitting passively to your partner without communicating your wants or needs.

These three types of responses (fight, flight or freeze) only perpetuate conflicts. Here we suggest a fourth response to conflict that allows you to integrate your differences with wisdom and mutual respect and thus resolve the conflict. We call it the **UVA response**. It is an acronym for: Understand, Value and Act. Obviously, conflicts caused not by legitimate differences but by pathological behaviors require professional therapy. However, most unresolved conflicts arise from the inability to integrate significant differences.

Here are some general guidelines for using the UVA approach:

1) You and your partner need to agree to address a conflict only when both of you are in control of your emotions, (even if you are still angry) and at a time that is mutually convenient.

2) The one who wants to address a specific conflict needs to define the conflict in behavioral terms. For example: "**When you**... (describe the problem behavior), **I feel**... (describe the emotional impact)." Then, he or she needs to offer a specific solution in concrete and positive terms. For example: "**In the future I would prefer that you**..." (Make a concrete, positive and realistic request).

3) The listener needs to provide a UVA response:

   a) **Understand** your partner's need or expectation. For example, "*Let me see if I understood your request. In the future you would prefer that I ..., is that correct?*" If your partner does not feel adequately understood, ask for further clarification.

   b) **Value** your partner's request even if you disagree with it (unless it is something immoral or illegal). When you value the request you are not saying that you agree with it but that you are willing to honor and respect what is important for your partner.

   c) **Act**: Commit to a specific behavioral change that addresses your partner's request. This is how you show your partner that you are committed to love him/her as he/she wants to be loved.

The UVA response is an empathic response that activates the cognitive (understand), emotional (value) and behavioral (act) dimensions of your love and facilitates the integration of your interpersonal differences. The couples who master this type of conflict resolution become strong and are able to maintain their unity in the midst of their diversity.

The following Conflict Resolution Questionnaire can help you and your partner identify your current use of the skills described in this chapter and it can be used as a tool for constructive dialogue on this key area of your marriage.

CONFLICT RESOLUTION SKILLS
QUESTIONNAIRE

Circle the answer which best describes how often you use these conflict resolution skills with your partner:

> 1 = Never
> 2 = A little
> 3 = Sometimes
> 4 = Pretty much
> 5 = A lot

1) Before I try to solve a conflict with my partner, I make sure that the two of us are in control of our emotions and that we are able to speak to each other respectfully:

1 2 3 4 5

2) When it is my turn to talk, I define the conflict using descriptive terms. For example: "*When you....I feel....*" (without blaming, criticizing or venting):

1 2 3 4 5

3) I state what I want or need in concrete and positive terms. For example: "*In the future, I would prefer that you...*" (without threats, complaints or asking for something unrealistic):

1 2 3 4 5

4) When it is my turn to listen, I make sure that I understand what my partner wants or needs from me. For example by asking him or her: *"Let me see if I understood you. In the future, you would prefer that I ..., is this correct?"*

1 2 3 4 5

5) I tell my partner that I value his or her request, even if I disagree with it, because I honor and respect him or her:

1 2 3 4 5

6) I commit to a specific and realistic behavior in response to my partner's request and out of love for him or her:

1 2 3 4 5

Before you try to solve a conflict,
make sure that you are in control of your emotions.

It is normal to feel frustrated, angry, anxious or depressed while going through a significant interpersonal conflict. The first step in dealing with the effects of the conflict is to regain emotional control without repressing your feelings. You can do this by replacing negative thoughts about the nature of the problem with positive thoughts about possible solutions. Watch out for the toxic thoughts that we described in chapter 6. They will only exacerbate your negative feelings. Replace them with their antidotes.

Some people find that engaging in a relaxing activity settles their emotions. Identify some activities that help you calm down and tell your partner that you need some time out before addressing the conflict. Be specific about the time you need so that your partner does not feel that you are avoiding him or her, or avoiding dealing with the conflict.

It is tempting to stop loving your partner until the conflict is resolved. Withdrawing love might be a natural response if you feel that your partner has hurt you, but deciding not to love will drain you emotionally and block the wisdom you need to find a solution. A solution not motivated by love will prove a temporary and unsatisfying compromise.

Define the conflict in behavioral terms.

Dwelling on the conflict, replaying it over and over in your head, ruminating about it, but failing to define it in behavioral terms will prevent its resolution. For example, focusing on your partner's irritating characteristics prevents you from recognizing what he or she actually may have done.

Assuming the motives of your partner can be another stumbling block. Assuming is a toxic thought that can lead to character assassination. If you define the conflict according to inaccurate assumptions about your partner's motives, you will hurt your partner and you will have created a much bigger conflict—lack of trust.

Define the solution in concrete, positive, and realistic terms.

One of the most common pitfalls when couples start talking about a conflict is to engage in venting negative feelings or complain and criticize without explaining clearly the behavioral changes needed to solve the conflict. Conflict resolution requires assertiveness from the speaker and empathy from the listener. Being assertive in this case means communicating a desired solution to a conflict in concrete, positive and realistic terms. Here is an example from a couple struggling with financial conflicts: "Honey, when you spend over $100 dollars without consulting with me I feel anxious about being able to pay all our bills. In the future I would prefer that you consult with me before you spend that kind of money." Assertiveness eliminates the need to vent, complain or criticize and invites the listener to engage in an empathic response.

Understand your partner's need or expectation.

It is not uncommon for a listener to misinterpret a request or to listen selectively only to parts of it or to distort a message with the bias of past negative experiences. The best way to make sure that your partner has been understood by you is by asking a question, using your own words, to verify that you have heard the message correctly. In the previous example of a couple with financial management conflicts, when the husband was asked to share what he understood that the wife was asking him, he replied: "She just wants to control me."

After further clarifications, he asked her: "Are you saying that from now on, if I want to spend over $100 dollars you would like me to consult with you first and decide together if we can afford it?" When she replied "yes!" he knew then that she felt understood.

Value your partner's request
even if you disagree with it.

This is one of the most challenging steps in conflict resolution because people do not feel like validating a request if they do not agree with it. In reality we can disagree with our partner's request but still honor it because we value him or her and because we value strengthening the relationship. Obviously, we never have to validate immoral or illegal requests but this is very rarely the case.

When we value our partner's request we show our respect, compassionate acceptance and willingness to integrate our differences in thinking styles, emotional sensitivities, values or behavioral preferences. In the previous example, the husband struggled to validate his wife's request because he preferred his individualistic approach regarding their finances but eventually he realized that he was disregarding his wife's needs and freely stated: "If this is important to you, then it is important to me too. I care about you." At that moment she felt validated.

Commit to a new behavior
relevant to your partner's request.

When we are willing to try a new behavior requested by our partner, we show concretely that we are committed to love our partner the way that he or she wants to be loved. This is the hallmark of empathy or intelligent love and one of the most effective ways to successfully resolve a conflict. At times our partner may ask for something that is not realistic, in that case our response should not be to reject the request but to adapt it to our possibilities. Instead of saying "sorry but that is not possible for me," it is better to say "I would like to honor your request and at this time the best that I can do is...." Any meaningful response should be welcomed as a step in the right direction. In the previous example, both husband and wife became better partners in their financial management as they made improvements towards their desired goal. It takes time to master the UVA response but the rewards are worth the effort. Conflict resolution is not only about solving conflicts but above all about integrating our differences and growing in mutual love.

Practice Assertiveness

What would you say if we told you that from now on you will never need to complain about or criticize your partner? We are not implying that you should bite the bullet and repress your anger; on the contrary we are saying that complaining and criticizing are ineffective ways to communicate how you want to be treated. The next time you feel tempted to complain or criticize, practice assertiveness.

Assertiveness is much more than affirming yourself verbally in a direct and confident manner. **The main purpose of assertiveness is to develop a better relationship with your partner by communicating clearly how you would like to be treated**. It eliminates the need to complain or to be critical, which only tells her or him what to avoid. Instead, it focuses on "coaching" the other on how you want to be loved. There are three basic steps to interpersonal coaching:

1) Practice compassionate acceptance

When you are upset with your partner it is easy to become critical and pass a negative judgment in your mind. Once you dwell on a negative thought you will experience a negative emotion (e.g., resentment, anxiety, sadness, etc.) which is often expressed with negative language or some negative behaviors. To break this destructive cycle, you can practice replacing negative judgments with compassionate acceptance. This means to accept your partner's current level of functioning (i.e., imperfections, mistakes, limitations, etc.) without becoming judgmental. Acceptance does not mean agreement, approval or avoidance. *It means loving unconditionally and having reality-based expectations*. This creates the necessary foundation to proceed to the next step in interpersonal coaching: the assertive communication of what you need or want from your partner.

2) Use assertive language

When you have removed negative judgments from your mind and subsequently removed also negative emotions from your heart, it is easier to articulate your needs or wishes using positive and invitational language. For example: "In the future I would prefer if you... (define a specific positive behavior)." Assertive language is a respectful, intelligent and engaging way of communicating how you would like to be treated. It has to be invitational language without hidden threats, guilt trips, or sarcastic remarks. It is solution-focused, behaviorally defined and it targets gradual improvement in your partner. *It tells your partner what you want instead of what you do not want*. It is based on your partner's current level of functioning not on your wishful thinking.

Without compassionate acceptance, you might make the mistake of venting, complaining or criticizing in order to communicate your needs. This type of critical language may result in your partner feeling condemned, rejected or devalued and it may contribute to an escalation of the conflict or your partner becoming avoidant and emotionally detached.

3) Appreciate progress

The last step is to pay attention and appreciate any observable progress in your partner in response to your assertive request. It works best when you let your partner know about the positive feelings that you have experienced (e.g., happy, grateful, encouraged, reassured, comforted, etc.) when (s)he did what you requested. It is very important to reinforce any visible progress versus withholding your appreciation until you have observed a major improvement. *The goal is gradual improvement not an extreme makeover.* Avoid giving a "performance review" which places you in a superior position and may be perceived as condescending.

An easy way to summarize these three steps is: *accept, assert and appreciate!*

Diffuse Criticism

Nobody likes to be criticized or to have one's competence and motives questioned but at some point, your partner is going to make critical remarks about you. How should you respond to your partner's criticism? Diffuse it. The next time that your partner criticizes you, instead of defending yourself ask, "What was your expectation?"

Your partner will criticize you when you have not met his or her expectations. *If you start defending yourself you are focusing on the wrong person.* Focus on what your partner wants or needs from you. Once you have understood your partner's expectation, do a reality check. If the expectation is legitimate, acknowledge it and explain how you are going to meet it. If it is unrealistic, respond to it in realistic terms.

You do not have to fulfill every wish from your partner. Diffusing criticism does not mean having to please your partner to satisfy your need for approval, or to avoid conflict. Discern whether your partner's need is genuine, whether or not you can give your partner what he or she wants, and when you would be available.

Can you imagine how many unnecessary conflicts and stressful experiences can be prevented by learning how to diffuse criticism and by practicing assertiveness? Couples tell us that these two skills alone have turned their marriages from a tense battlefield into a peaceful partnership. These are powerful skills because they allow you to focus on positive behaviors that need to be developed, while maintaining a high level of respect for each other.

DIFFUSING CRITICISM EXERCISE

1) Identify a personal criticism from your partner that made you defensive and find an appropriate moment to ask your partner the following:

"I am sorry that you felt upset about _____.
Please tell me, what was your expectation?"

2) Respond to that expectation in a realistic and fair manner. If the expectation is legitimate, acknowledge it and tell your partner:

"Thank you for explaining what you want. This is
what I could do _____ and this is when I could
do it _____". Be specific.

If you find the expectation to be unrealistic, tell your partner what would be realistic for you.

3) Complete your feedback by telling your partner calmly:

"The next time you do not need to criticize me.
Just tell me what you want."

11. The Power to Forgive and Reconcile

Sooner or later a failure to love or some unfair behavior will cause pain in a marriage. When that happens, activate the power of forgiveness. Partners who have suffered from abuse or have felt victimized by their partner's unfaithfulness, however, need to seek professional help.

Forgiveness is not something extraordinary reserved for special moments, but a part of daily life. It is unrealistic to expect that partners will always love each other perfectly and will never say or do anything offensive. Unity is a dynamic process that requires constant and mutual self-giving. It goes without saying that sometimes this process is interrupted. Forgiveness is essential to building unity between partners. It allows you to be real, to accept each other completely, and to restore unity whenever it has been broken.

There are many misconceptions about forgiveness. Forgiveness is not condoning, excusing or justifying an injustice. When you forgive you seek to integrate mercy with justice by naming the injustice and asking for a genuine and visible change in your partner.

Forgiveness is not avoiding a conflict with your partner and moving on. The only way to move ahead is by transforming your relationship, not by avoiding the issue or detaching from your partner.

Forgiveness is not becoming indifferent or anesthetizing your feelings. It requires that you honor your feelings and restore them by healing the relationship with your partner.

Forgiveness is not a sign of personal weakness. It takes a great deal of courage to confront an injustice and to work hard at overcoming evil with good.

Forgiveness is not a solitary act but a healing journey that involves your soul, mind, heart, and will. It is a transformation of the way your see your partner, your response to his or her offense, and your relationship.

Forgive with Your Soul

To forgive is to love as God loves. In God, love and mercy coincide. God loves you always, takes the initiative in showing his love for you, and embraces you as you are. His mercy restores your dignity as a child of God. The strength and the motivation to forgive your partner come from the fact that God has forgiven you; God expects you to do the same with your partner.

When you forgive your partner with your soul you are saying: **"Who you are is more important than what you did."** You can fill any absence of love from your partner with an act of pure love. As the great mystic John of the Cross has written, "Wherever there is no love, put love and you will find love." If the Spirit of God lives in you, you can be compassionate as God is compassionate.

Forgive with Your Mind

Sometimes, your mind might dwell obsessively on an offense and toxic thoughts might feed your anger, anxiety, or sadness. Replace your toxic thoughts with their antidotes as described in chapter 6. Pay special attention to toxic thoughts such as negative bias, all or nothing, assuming, and emotional reasoning.

Focus your mind on what you value about your partner and your marriage and think about the behavioral changes necessary to overcome the injustice that has arisen. Think about some relevant and specific behaviors that your partner could do to heal the relationship.

Whenever your mind goes back to the offense, redirect it to the present and to the new behaviors needed to build a better relationship. You cannot forgive your partner with your heart if you do not forgive him or her first with your mind.

Forgive with Your Heart

Cancel the emotional debt. Forgiveness is always possible. You need not consider whether you can forgive but whether you want to forgive. Forgiving with your heart means removing any lingering resentment through an act of mercy and refusing to use the offense as a weapon against your partner.

Expressing anger does not eliminate it; solving the injustice does. At times you might be tempted to wait for your anger to dissipate before you decide to forgive your partner. Time does not solve or heal anything; people do.

Your anger will decrease and even disappear when you restore the dignity of your partner in your soul with an act of pure mercy, identify the new behaviors necessary to promote justice, and freely decide to do your part to reconcile with your partner. If your partner does his or her part and your rapport is renewed and strengthened, your anger will be replaced with joy and peace.

No matter how much anger you feel, you can always choose how to treat your partner. You are free to do your part to promote mercy and justice. You can do this if you live in the present moment and if you continue to invest in healthy relationships that can provide you with emotional support when you most need it.

Forgiveness will never make you emotionally bankrupt; on the contrary, the more you forgive, the greater the supply of compassionate love in your heart.

Forgive with Your Will

The last stage on the journey of forgiveness consists in making the decision and taking the initiative to reconcile. Invite your partner to make the necessary changes to heal and build a better relationship. Reconciliation is not "fixing" the old relationship with your partner but building a new one. Married life is like building a new house day by day, not buying a "fixer upper" and spending the rest of your life solving one problem after another. Obviously this requires willingness from both of you. Reconciliation is the mature fruit of forgiveness that integrates mercy and justice and allows your love to become stronger.

The commitment to forgive is a decision that can occur even if you are still feeling angry and resentful. You can make that decision if you realize that you do not have to act on your resentment and that you have control over how to respond to your partner's offense.

Once you have made your decision to forgive and reconcile, communicate it to your partner in a respectful and engaging manner. Then articulate your expectations about what he or she needs to do to reach a genuine reconciliation.

When you forgive with your will, you complete a healing journey of forgiveness that matures and purifies your love and renews and strengthens your marriage.

If your partner resists or refuses your attempt to reconcile, seek professional help before you decide to end your marriage. The journey from forgiveness to reconciliation can be filled with obstacles that require help to be overcome.

The Forgiveness Exercise that follows outlines a process that you can use whenever you need to activate the journey from forgiveness to reconciliation. Fill it out and discuss your answers with your partner.

FORGIVENESS EXERCISE

Write down an unresolved injustice that you have suffered from your partner. (Define it according to what happened, not based on how you felt. Be specific and brief.)

Did you restore the dignity of your partner in your soul? ("Who you are is more important than what you did.")

What behavioral changes do you need from your partner to build a new and better relationship? (Mention specific behaviors. Seek improvement, not perfection.)

Did you cancel all the emotional debt and are you living in the present?

Express your forgiveness to your partner and state the behavioral changes necessary for a meaningful reconciliation.

If you are the one who offended your partner, have the humility to ask for forgiveness. Indicate the behavioral changes that you are going to make, to the best of your abilities, to prevent it from happening again. Do not justify your unfair behavior or blame your partner for it; pride can bias your reasoning and create an obstacle to reconciliation.

12. The Soul of Mutuality

Throughout the centuries, Christian spiritualities have had one of two emphases: the presence of God within one's soul, or the presence of God in one's neighbor. Those spiritualities illuminate what we have called the soul of autonomy and the soul of empathy respectively. Now, at the beginning of the third millennium, we are entering a new stage in understanding Christian spirituality. In addition to the previous approaches there is a new focal point: the presence of Jesus in the midst of the Christian community. We draw our inspiration for the soul of mutuality from the writings of Chiara Lubich, whose spirituality of unity is lived by millions of Christians and people from other faith traditions all over the world.

How can you live a spirituality of unity in your marriage? In addition to loving Jesus in your partner and letting Jesus grow within you as we described in chapters 4 and 8, respectively, you need to promote mutual love to experience the presence of Jesus in your midst: *"Where*

121

two or three are united in my name, there am I in the midst of them" (Matthew 18:20).

The presence of Jesus between you and your partner is the soul of mutuality. To have him present you need to make a daily commitment to love each other as your first priority, to share what you have and who you are, and to forgive and reconcile as needed.

Put Mutual Love First

Before anything else, your first priority should always be to love your partner. This is a simple yet radical commitment. This is what you agreed to do when you married each other. This is important because your mutual love will generate the most precious reality: Jesus among you. He is more valuable and more important than anything else that you can do or possess.

Unfortunately, it is easy to lose this focus to worries about work, finances, health problems, parenting issues, and so on. Whenever you become task-oriented or shift to a problem-solving mode and forget to love your partner, your life and your relationship become burdensome and draining. Love can never be taken for granted; it is like a fire that needs to be fed constantly.

Share What You Have and Who You Are

Mutuality is nurtured by sharing what you have and who you are. It is tempting to become attached to things and to create artificial boundaries to protect your possessions. Mutual love in marriage translates to "whatever is mine is yours" and vice versa. That means everything:

car, computer, closet space, bank account, remote control, every room in the house, everything.

Sharing is not limited to what you have but also includes who you are: your inner life, whatever gives meaning and purpose to your life, your soul. This is perhaps one of the greatest gaps in marriages today. The amount and quality of couples' communication leaves so much to be desired. Rarely do couples share their spiritual lives with each other. Not sharing your soul deprives your partner of your greatest treasure.

Generally, we eat breakfast and dinner as a family. During that time we share our experiences of how we have lived the gospel. We do it with simplicity and spontaneity. It is always enjoyable and inspiring. We do not want our spiritual life to be artificial, something reserved only for church on Sunday. Rather, we want it to permeate and give meaning to everything that we do every day. We have noticed that the more we share our souls the greater our unity becomes.

Make a Pact of Mercy

Certainly, there will be moments when you do not love each other. It is critical to know what to do when that happens. To be able to start again whenever there is a lack of unity with your partner, you need a merciful heart. You can transform your heart of stone into a heart rich in compassion by establishing a pact of mercy with your partner.

Every night, before you fall asleep, forgive whatever grievance you might have against your partner. As we described in chapter 11, you start this process by restoring your partner's dignity in your soul. Eliminate any toxic thoughts (judgments) about your partner and think about the behavioral changes needed to improve any painful situation. Finally, *cancel all the emotional debt* in your heart and refuse to hold any grudges. It is as if you burn everything in a fire of mercy. When you wake up the next day, look at your partner with new eyes, without dwelling in the past. At an appropriate moment, talk with your partner about the behavioral changes needed to improve your relationship. This process will allow you both to experience the joy of reconciliation.

This pact of mercy removes any impurities that might have crept into your relationship during the day and promotes healing and growth. An act of mercy is a shot of pure love that renews and revitalizes your marriage.

The Key to Unity

We have mentioned three ways to promote mutuality and unity in your marriage. When you love each other as Jesus loved you, he is present in your midst and he makes you one. Unity is possible only if Jesus is present among you. Jesus came to earth precisely with this goal in mind. The night before he died, he revealed his innermost desire when he expressed his last will and testament in his prayer to his Father: "That they may be one, as we are one" (John 17:22).

How did he obtain unity for us? He gave us his life on the cross, but even more, he experienced total abandonment. To reunite us with God and with one another he first had to experience everything that separated us. This moment of mysterious abandonment took place when he cried out: "*My God, my God, why have you forsaken me?*" (Matthew 27:46). How did he overcome that tragic experience of lack of unity? He transformed it into an act of love that only he could have done. He entrusted himself completely to his Father's love: "*Father, into your hands I commend my spirit*" (Luke 23:46). Jesus obtained our unity with God and with one another through his abandonment on the cross and subsequent death and resurrection. Any form of Christian unity, including marriage, is achieved through our love for Jesus Forsaken. Unity and Jesus Forsaken are intrinsically linked; we cannot understand and live one without the other.

Jesus Forsaken Is Our Standard of Empathy

We have described empathy as the process of emptying yourself to become one with your partner and responding meaningfully to your partner's needs. In his abandonment on the cross, Jesus emptied himself of everything to become one with us and to give us what we need most: our relationship with God, as God's children, and our unity with one another as true brothers and sisters.

Whenever you practice empathy, think of him as the model and measure of your love for your partner. Empty yourself completely, as he did, to make room inside yourself for your partner. Accept everything that your partner lives and make it yours, as Jesus did. Discern what your partner needs and give it without holding anything back, as he did.

Jesus Forsaken Is Our Standard of Autonomy

Autonomy maximizes your ability to love and become a gift to your partner. In his abandonment, Jesus demonstrates the ultimate standard for the measure of our love. He gave himself completely and freely. In that moment, for the first time in his life, he did not feel the love of his Father. He made a free choice to love the Father even though he did not feel the Father's love in return. At that moment, he was the first one to love. He is our model in taking the initiative to love concretely and to the end.

As you seek to live autonomy, think of him as your model. Be the first to love, as he did. See your life as a gift for your partner, and spend it loving concretely and to the end, as he did.

Jesus Forsaken Is Our Standard of Mutuality

Mutuality is the result of seeking unity above anything else, sharing everything, and forgiving everything. Jesus experienced his abandonment precisely because of the lack of unity between us and God. He loved us to the point of becoming one with us completely. Even though he had committed no sin he became sin, and therefore abandoned. "For our sakes God made him who did not know sin, to be sin, so that in him we might become the very holiness of God" (2 Corinthians 5:21).

His deepest desire in life was to make us one with God and with one another. That was always his first priority and the underlying motivation behind everything that he said or did. He could only achieve this unity by means of a love that passed through his abandonment; otherwise he would have chosen another way. He said "No one has a greater love than the one who lays down his life for his friends" (John 15:13). On the cross he gives us not only his physical life, but above all his divine life. In his abandonment he gives us his Spirit; with us, Jesus shares who he is.

Through his abandonment, his forgiveness restores our dignity as children of God and cancels all our debts. He invites us to do the same and to reconcile with each other.

To promote mutuality with your partner, keep one goal in mind: seek unity with your partner above anything else. When you share, share what you have and who you are, as he did. Forgive everything as he did, restoring always the dignity of your partner.

Divine Alchemy: The Secret of Lasting Happiness

There is a way to transform every negative into a positive. Every life contains physical, emotional or spiritual pain. This form of suffering cannot be eliminated, but it can be transformed and made manageable and meaningful.

First, eliminate those forms of suffering that you have inflicted on yourself. You can change unhealthy ways of thinking or acting as we have discussed in chapters 5, 6 and 7. When experiences of suffering occur that you did not cause, you have four possible responses: you can fight them, try to flee from them, remained paralyzed by them, or transform them. The first three approaches will only perpetuate or even increase the suffering.

How can we transform suffering? Christians believe that Jesus took upon himself all forms of suffering caused by sin and redeemed them on the cross. We have used

the term Jesus Forsaken to describe precisely that
moment in his life when he took upon himself every
human suffering, be it physical, emotional, or spiritual.
He transformed all forms of suffering into love by
entrusting himself completely to his Father. The Father's
response was the Resurrection. If you embrace and love
Jesus in every suffering, he will lead you through the
same process of divine alchemy that he went through.
Jesus Forsaken becomes your point of entry into an exis-
tential encounter with the Trinity.

In this encounter you first meet Jesus, present in your
suffering. Every form of suffering contains him because
he became that suffering on the cross. Whenever you are
hurting, name your suffering and believe that Jesus is
present in that painful situation. For example, when you
feel lonely, embrace him who became loneliness so that
you will never be alone again; when you feel anxious,
embrace him who became anxiety to give you reassurance; when you feel depressed, embrace him who
became depression to comfort you; when you feel division, embrace him who became division to unite you;
when you feel sin, embrace him who became sin to give
you God's grace; when you feel darkness, embrace him
who became darkness to give you light; when you feel
desperate, embrace him who became despair to give you
hope; when you feel like a total failure, embrace him
who became failure to give you victory over every
personal struggle. Name your own suffering, and if you
embrace Jesus in your suffering he will reveal himself to
you.

Embracing Jesus in suffering is not a spiritual gimmick
to avoid dealing with a painful situation. On the
contrary, it is the most honest and mature way to face
and overcome suffering. It is an encounter with Jesus as
the redeemer of every suffering. Choose to embrace him

in suffering initially with your will; over the years, however, you will notice that your choice will also come from your heart. When you encounter him in suffering, tell Jesus, "I am happy to love you as you loved me."

Do not waste time analyzing the suffering or waiting until you can feel his presence. You will never understand Jesus Forsaken by thinking about it, only by loving him. If you love him so that the pain will go away you are not loving him but only using him to get rid of the pain. Your encounter with him is real when you have no ulterior motives and you rejoice to become one with him.

Next, you encounter the Father. Jesus himself will lead you to him and invite you to do what he did: entrust all your concerns to the Father. At this moment you relinquish your suffering and your control over it to him, with complete faith in his love for you. You abandon yourself to the Father's love, believing that whatever he wants or allows to happen will be the best thing for you because that will bring you closest to him. At times this requires heroic faith. Your own experience will show you that the Father will never be outdone in love and you will receive the profound peace of knowing that your life is in the best possible hands, those of a Father who did not hesitate to spare his own son out of love for you.

Finally, you encounter the Holy Spirit. After you have entrusted your suffering to the Father and you have decided to love God by doing God's will or to love the person next to you in that moment, you will experience a new presence of the Holy Spirit within you. The Spirit will give you a special gift of joy. You need not postpone loving until the suffering has been resolved or until your painful feelings have dissipated. At the moment you decide to love and not dwell on yourself, you will experience the divine alchemy of passing from death to life. "We have passed from death to life because we have loved" (1 John 3:14). When you start loving God and others, you will experience a new life within you: the presence of the Holy Spirit.

Once you start loving again, your pain will become manageable or disappear and you will feel transformed and renewed by the presence of the Holy Spirit within. Your heart will fill with a joy and peace that nothing and nobody can take away from you.

The encounter with Jesus in our suffering, with the Father as we entrust our suffering to him, and with the Holy Spirit as we activate our love in the present moment is a spiritual process that at first may take a long time. As we mature spiritually, it can happen in a matter of seconds.

You will discover that suffering is no longer to be feared or avoided. It provides the golden opportunity for an intimate encounter with God that transforms suffering into love for God and others. This is the secret of Christian joy, of that endless happiness for which every human being thirsts. This joy, a gift of the Holy Spirit, is present whenever we love Jesus Forsaken as he loved us. This experience of divine alchemy is simple yet profound. We can never thank Jesus enough for what he did and what he shared in his abandonment.

Loving Jesus Forsaken is the key
to our unity with God
and with each other,
and the secret for authentic happiness.

By living the model of Christian marriage that we have shared in this book, you and your partner will experience the fullness of joy that Jesus promised when you are united.

If you would like to learn more about what you have read or share how it has helped you and your marriage, we would love to hear from you. For information on contacting us, see "The Authors" at the end of the book.

Acknowledgments

We thank God for showing us that the heart and soul of Christian marriage contains the same dynamic of love as that lived within the Trinity, a relationship that is possible on earth wherever two are united in Jesus' name.

We express our gratitude to our parents, whose testimony of faithful love has given us the foundation to discover love's endless possibilities in our own marriage.

We also offer particular thanks to Chiara Lubich, whose spirituality of unity has guided our spiritual journey and has given us the opportunity to integrate contemporary spirituality with our own psychological expertise.

Our psychological perspective has benefited greatly from the significant contributions to the field of marital research by authors such as John Gottman, Andrew Christensen, Neil Jacobson, Howard Markman, Clifford Notarius, Scott Stanley, and Gayla Margolin, with whom John studied at the University of Southern California.

Above all, we owe a debt to every couple with whom we have worked for the last thirty years in our private practice and in our workshops. We have learned from each of them and this book is a tribute to the collective wisdom gathered from those meaningful and at times difficult encounters. Thanks to them this book is not filled with our opinions or with theoretical advice. Their feedback about renewed and happier marriages has motivated us to write. Many of them asked us the same question: "When are you going to write a book about all these things that we have learned here?" For years we kept answering: "Soon." Finally, here it is.

We thank all those who have invited us to work with marriage and family ministries and who offer our programs through the offices of Family Life and Religious Education of many dioceses in the U.S., the National Association of Catholic Family Life Ministers, Marriage Encounter, Engaged Encounter, Retrouvaille, New Families Movement, Movimiento Familiar Cristiano, and numerous churches from various denominations with whom we are honored to serve as consultants.

Our friend, Linda Frantom, introduced us to each other and has accompanied the adventure of our marriage from its beginning. We treasure her friendship and her sharing of her own beautiful journey.

One person in particular has scrutinized how the authors practice what they teach and write: our son, Paul. He has attended many of our presentations and has volunteered observations and timely reminders with disarming grace. He has adapted to our schedules and professional responsibilities with unusual patience and generosity. He has provided us with a constant "reality check" and, at times, even served as our "in-house theologian." For example, once he overheard us discussing the fact that some couples get discouraged when a negative event occurs between them because they think that it erases their previous positive experiences. When we commented that the negative does not necessarily erase the positive, he quickly added, "yes, but even more important than that is the fact that the positive can erase the negative." When we asked him what he meant, he said simply, "Because good can conquer evil." His comments reminded us that happiness is not the result of decreasing the negative but of promoting the positive. You will read more about this in chapter 6.

We acknowledge the editorial expertise of Tom Masters and the collaboration and professionalism of Gary Brandl and the staff at New City Press.

Finally, we want to thank you, our readers. We hope that this book provides a relevant, inspirational, practical and effective tool for renewing your marriage.

The Authors

Dr. John Yzaguirre, licensed psychologist, consultant, and author, specializes in marriage and family life enrichment and the integration of psychology and Christian spirituality. He has developed successful prevention and intervention programs at mental health agencies in Boston, New York, Los Angeles and Orange County. A native of Barcelona, Spain, he has offered his psychological services in the United States for over 30 years and is a former director of the psychology department at Children's Hospital of Orange County. He has been a keynote speaker at international and national conventions in the United States, Europe, Mexico, and Australia. Dr. Yzaguirre received his Master's degree in Psychology from Boston College, and his doctorate in psychology from the University of Southern California.

Claire Frazier-Yzaguirre, M.Div., M.F.T., is a licensed marriage and family therapist, a formally ordained American Baptist minister, and a marriage and family life consultant, assisting churches in the development and growth of their marriage and family life ministries, women's ministries, Christian leadership and faith formation. She has over 30 years of professional experience helping couples and families. As an ordained minister she has developed programs for campus ministry, church ministries, marriage and family ministries, lay leadership formation and community outreach. She spent one year at the Institute of Holy Land Studies, Jerusalem, specializing in biblical studies and ecumenical dialogue. She has been invited to speak on marriage and family life at churches and conventions throughout the United States. She holds Master's degrees from Fuller School of Psychology and from Fuller School of Theology in Pasadena, CA.

John and Claire currently maintain their clinical practice in Irvine, California. Every year in 50+ cities, they present their Thriving Marriages programs to thousands of couples, people and faith leaders involved in Marriage and Family life, Religious Education and Adult Faith Formation ministries helping them grow more thriving, resilient, and compassionate families and faith communities.

You can contact them at:

2081 Business Center Dr., Ste. 170
Irvine, CA 92612
(949) 851-1572
cfy@cox.net
www.ThrivingFamilies.com

NEW CITY PRESS
of the Focolare
Hyde Park, New York

New City Press is one of more than 20 publishing houses sponsored by the Focolare, a movement founded by Chiara Lubich to help bring about the realization of Jesus' prayer: "That all may be one" (John 17:21). In view of that goal, New City Press publishes books and resources that enrich the lives of people and help all to strive toward the unity of the entire human family. We are a member of the Association of Catholic Publishers.

Further Reading

Thriving Marriages is also available in a Spanish Edition.
Casados y felices   978-1-56548-218-0 $12.95

Visit www.newcitypress.com for more titles on family life.

Periodicals
Living City Magazine,
www.livingcitymagazine.com

Scan to join our mailing list for discounts and promotions

or go to

www.newcitypress.com

and click on "join our email list."